Christianity and
American Freemasonry

WILLIAM J. WHALEN

THE BRUCE PUBLISHING COMPANY
MILWAUKEE

NIHIL OBSTAT:

JOHN A. SCHULIEN
Censor librorum

IMPRIMATUR:

✠ ALBERTUS G. MEYER
Archiepiscopus Milwauchiensis
die 21ª Augusti, 1958

I have my doubts about this Book

Library of Congress Catalog Card Number: 58–13622

© 1958 THE BRUCE PUBLISHING COMPANY
MADE IN THE UNITED STATES OF AMERICA
(Fourth Printing — 1961)

PREFACE

This book has been written to explain why the Church has warned her sons against affiliating with the Masonic lodge since 1738. The Christian case against the lodge is conclusive. We need not prove the existence of a grand conspiracy in which American Freemasons participate nor need we resort to the bag of old wives' tales which circulate among some Catholics. We will simply show that a Christian cannot divide his allegiance between Jesus Christ and the Grand Architect of the Universe.

This is the first full-length treatment of this subject by an American Catholic in 50 years. A few pamphlets and magazine articles have appeared now and then since Arthur Preuss published *A Study in American Freemasonry* in 1908. Later Mr. Preuss included Freemasonry in his *Dictionary of Secret and Other Societies* which appeared in 1924.

Several excellent books by English writers in this field have been published in recent years, namely, *Darkness Visible* and *Christian by Degrees*, by Walton Hannah, then an Anglican priest and now a student for the Roman Catholic priesthood at the Beda in Rome, and *The Nature of Freemasonry* by Dr. Hubert S. Box, also an Anglican. Both are valuable additions to the literature, thoroughly reliable but mainly concerned with English Masonry.

We have not undertaken this present study in order to irritate members of the lodge nor to satisfy the mere curiosity of non-Masons. On the other hand, we have felt no compulsion to award Masonry that immunity from criticism which it seems to expect in this country.

In so far as possible we have allowed Masons to speak for themselves in this volume. We have relied heavily on the two foremost authorities in American Freemasonry: Albert Pike and Dr. Albert

G. Mackey. Pike remodeled the entire structure of the Scottish rite and served as Sovereign Grand Commander of the Southern jurisdiction from 1859 until his death in 1891. Mackey furnished the Craft with a library of basic books including his *Encyclopedia of Freemasonry*, *The Symbolism of Freemasonry*, *Mackey's Masonic Ritualist*, *A Lexicon of Freemasonry*, and a *Textbook of Masonic Jurisprudence*. No one in the history of the lodge in the United States has had more influence and prestige than these two men.

Mackey erred, however, when he wrote in his *Encyclopedia* (p. 617), "The truth is that men who are not Masons never read authentic Masonic works. They have no interest in the topics discussed, and could not understand them, from a want of the preparatory education which the Lodge alone can supply. Therefore, were a writer even to trench a little on what may be considered as being really the *arcana* of Masonry, there is no danger of his thus making an improper revelation to improper persons." On the contrary this "improper" person has long had an interest in the topics discussed and has discovered innumerable corroborative bits of evidence in Masonic monitors, encyclopedias, speeches, commentaries, lectures, and histories.

Besides the writings of Masons and critics of Masonry, we have consulted the various exposés written by disgruntled and disillusioned Masons. These range from the original American exposé of Captain Morgan through that of Evangelist and Oberlin college president Charles Finney to modern revelations including those of Protestant ministers who have renounced the lodge. With the proper precautions these exposés can be of considerable value even though Masonic publications follow the simple policy of flatly denying their authenticity and impugning the integrity of the defectors. The trivial variations among the rituals of the 49 states and the District of Columbia can be produced to discredit before naïve brethren any particular pirated ritual.

Masons themselves own and use little cipher books which present the degree workings in a simple cryptography — much easier to decipher than most crossword puzzles. These can be obtained by mail from Masonic publishers for $3.50 a copy or purchased without show of credentials at most large bookstores. One Lutheran minister has translated such rituals, known as *Ecce Orienti* or *King Solomon's Temple*, for 40 of the 49 states. Furthermore, unsympathetic or careless widows of members are likely to offer their husbands' Masonic libraries to secondhand dealers and booksellers and some such collections have even found their way to the shelves of Catholic university libraries. Negro Masons who belong to lodges which white Masons brand as "clandestine" have no difficulty in obtaining genuine rituals for their own use. If there is one secret in Masonry it is that there are no Masonic secrets.

Finally, we have obtained the wholehearted co-operation of three former Masons who are now active Catholic laymen. Two of these men were 32nd degree members in the Scottish rite and one served as Worshipful Master of his lodge. The third reached the Order of Knights Templar in the York rite. Each has checked the chapters on the Blue Lodge initiation and on the Scottish and York rites. We have agreed to spare them any possible harassment by their former brethren by not divulging their names. Their assistance, however, is deeply appreciated.

Dr. Paul M. Bretscher of Concordia Seminary in St. Louis, chairman of the Commission on Fraternal Organizations of the Lutheran Church-Missouri Synod, graciously consented to review the entire manuscript. His suggestions and comments have been invaluable. I would also like to thank Walton Hannah, Fr. John A. Hardon, S.J., Fr. Leo Piguet, Pastor Harold F. Roellig, and Pastor E. P. Weber.

The following copyright holders have given permission for the use of quotations and I am happy to acknowledge my indebtedness to them: Britons Publishing Society, Chapman and Hall, Ltd., Concordia Publishing House, David McKay Co., *Ebony*, Encyclopedia Americana, Harper and Brothers, George G. Harrap and Co., Ltd., Alfred A. Knopf, Inc., *Look Magazine*, Dr. Norman Vincent Peale, A. D. Peters, Philosophical Library, Charles T. Powner, and the Watchtower Bible and Tract Society of New York, Inc. I would also like to thank my wife for her encouragement and for assistance in typing.   **W. J. W.**

CONTENTS

CHRISTIANITY AND
AMERICAN FREEMASONRY

"No man cometh to the Father, but by me."
Jn. 14:6

CHAPTER I

AMERICAN FREEMASONRY

Majority of World's Masons Live in the United States

One out of every dozen American men belongs to the Masonic order, largest and oldest secret fraternal society. These 4,100,000 men belong to a lodge which has come under the severest condemnation of the Roman Catholic Church since 1738. Any Catholic who affiliates with the Masonic lodge is automatically excommunicated, forfeits any share in the public prayers of the Church, and is denied a Christian burial; any Mason who wishes to enter the Church must sever all ties with the lodge.

Masons as well as Catholics know of the historic antagonism between the two societies, Church and lodge, but few seem to know the reasons for the attitude of the Church. Some Masons attribute the Church's ban to some musty political quarrel or imagine that the ban has something to do with the confessional. Too many Catholics are content to know that the Church forbids membership in the lodge without bothering to investigate the reasons behind this absolute prohibition.

The majority of American Masons, joining the lodge for business or social reasons and advancing no further than the basic Blue Lodge, seldom display that violent hatred of Catholicism which characterizes their Latin brethren. These "Knife and Fork" Masons demonstrate no particular interest in the philosophical and esoteric

1

aspects of Freemasonry and consider the lodge simply a mutual benefit and friendly society.

Actually, only those Masons in the Scottish rite, Southern jurisdiction, are exposed to a systematic vilification of the Church and many of these are too fair minded to judge Catholicism by the distortions of the New Age. Many Masons in the United States entertain kindly feelings toward the Catholic Church, support its hospitals and social welfare institutions, and may even enroll their children in parochial schools and Catholic colleges and universities. They see no reason why the Church should single out their lodge for condemnation since they avoid discussing religion in the lodge room, open their Temples to men of all faiths, and try to live good Christian lives themselves. They are usually convinced that the popes have been misled regarding the nature of Anglo-Saxon Freemasonry and that the excommunication should apply only to Catholics who join the admittedly political and anticlerical Grand Orients. They see no essential differences between their lodge and the local Knights of Columbus council and wonder if this is not just another example of clerical intolerance.

These men of good will deserve a calm explanation of the position of the Church. We will attempt to outline the chief reasons for the drastic penalty which the Church attaches to lodge membership and to explain why the Church as the divinely instituted guardian of faith and morals must oppose the basis of the Masonic system. A chapter will be devoted to a survey of Latin and European Masonry but we will concentrate on the Masonic lodge in mid-century America.

Masons generally define Masonry as a system of morality veiled in allegory and illustrated by symbols. The chief allegory which forms the basis of the third or Master Mason's degree is that of Hiram Abiff. Hiram appears briefly in the Biblical description of the building of King Solomon's Temple but Masonry has added a legend about his assassination and burial which becomes the death and resurrection rite of the degree. Identified in the Bible as a worker in metals, he becomes a stonemason in Masonry. Mackey admits:

Hiram the Builder, therefore, and all that refers to the legend of his connection with the temple, and his fate — such as the sprig of acacia, the hill near Mount Moriah, and the lost word — are to be considered as belonging to the class of mythical or legendary symbols.[1]

In other words, Hiram Abiff as presented in the third degree has the same substance as Santa Claus. Masonry takes its symbols from the tool kit of the working mason: the square, the trowel, the compass, etc. The founders of modern Masonry might conceivably have chosen some other occupation such as printing or agriculture as their pattern but there were obvious symbolic advantages to masonry.

Modern Masonry dates from 1717 when four craft lodges gathered in a London tavern and set up a Constitution for Free and Accepted Masons. These nonworking or "honorary" Masons eventually took over the degenerate lodges of working masons and developed the system of speculative Masonry we know today. We will discuss the origin of the lodge at greater detail in the following chapter.

Today, some 240 years later, Masonry is firmly entrenched in the United States and the British Commonwealth and claims small constituencies in other countries. In many American communities, particularly in the South and Middle West, the local lodge forms a sort of pan-Protestant men's fellowship; membership in the lodge is considered a certificate of bourgeois respectability. As we shall see, a large number of Protestant and Eastern Orthodox bodies continue to oppose the lodge but the main Protestant denominations — Methodist, Baptist, Presbyterian, Episcopalian — offer no official objection to dual membership in the lodge and the Christian church. Unlike the traditionally anti-Semitic German lodges, the American lodges admit Jews and other non-Christians. The lodge demands only belief in God and in the immortality of the soul. Since these two landmarks were rejected by the French Grand Orient in 1877, the American and other Anglo-Saxon lodges withdrew formal recognition. American Freemasonry assumes a Christian disguise which enabled it to get a solid footing in a professedly

---

[1] Albert G. Mackey, *Symbolism of Freemasonry* (Chicago: Masonic History Co., 1946), p. 200.

Christian nation; its fundamental naturalism and deism would never have commended it to the children of the Puritans.

Masonic authorities are unable to agree on the precise number of "landmarks," the Masonic name for the essential points of the Craft. However, Anglo-Saxons usually include the following landmarks in any listing: the modes of recognition including signs, grips, and passwords, the three degree system including the Royal Arch, the Hiramic legend of the third degree, belief in a Supreme Architect and in a future life, the right of any Master Mason to visit any regular lodge, the use of the Volume of Sacred Law, the equality of all members of the lodge, secrecy, and the symbolic method of teaching.

Masonry bars most of mankind from its Temples. No women, minors, atheists, or cripples may enter into its secrets. President Franklin D. Roosevelt, a 32nd degree Mason, could not have been initiated after he was stricken with polio. Negroes are refused admittance to Caucasian lodges but they have organized their own parallel lodges, considered "clandestine" and irregular by white Masons.

The lodge disclaims political interests but everyone knows that in many communities Masonic backing can mean the difference between victory and defeat at the polls. The Scottish rite does not hold itself bound by the self-imposed Masonic gag on discussions of religion and politics in the lodge. Almost all non-Catholic professional politicians have taken the precaution of donning the white apron; some strengthen their lodge ties by joining the working class Odd Fellows and Knights of Pythias as well. A survey in 1942 revealed that 34 of the 48 state governors were Masons (including thirteen 32nd degree members and six 33rds) while 55 of 96 senators were also brethren. John Gunther describes the influence of the lodge in one Middle Western state:

> Another powerful element in Iowa is Masonry. Of 108 members of the lower house of the legislature, about seventy belong to the Masonic lodge, though nobody ever runs "as" a Mason, and only seldom is a man asked directly if he is one or not. Governor Blue is a Mason; so is the attorney general; so is every supreme court justice. Two things explain this: (1) Masonry is a kind of badge of

respectability, not only in Iowa but in almost all the Mississippi basin states; (2) A man comes up through the local Masonic lodge and, if he shows leadership, is pushed outward to the legislature almost as a matter of course.[2]

The importance of Masonic affiliation for the office seeker has led many people to believe the legend that only a Mason can become president of the United States. Investigation reveals that only 13 presidents have belonged to the lodge and of these one, Fillmore, recanted. The others were Washington, Jackson, Polk, Buchanan, Johnson, Garfield, McKinley, Theodore Roosevelt, Taft, Harding, Franklin D. Roosevelt, and Truman. American voters have been unable to cast a ballot for a Masonic presidential candidate since 1948; Eisenhower, Stevenson, Nixon, and Kennedy were all non-Masons.

Some chief executives have been bitter critics of secret societies. For example, John Quincy Adams wrote: "I am prepared to complete the demonstration before God and man, that the Masonic oath, obligations and penalties cannot possibly be reconciled to the laws of morality, of Christianity, or of the land." Fillmore, the ex-Mason, warned: "The Masonic fraternity tramples upon our rights, defeats the administration of justice, and bids defiance to every government which it cannot control."

Teddy Roosevelt joined the lodge only after he became vice-president; Taft, like Generals Marshall and MacArthur at a later date, was made a Mason "at sight" which meant that he did not have to undergo the regular initiation procedure. All Grand Masters have the prerogative of making Masons at sight but seldom exercise it. Harding became an Entered Apprentice in 1920 but opposition within his hometown lodge prevented his further advancement. By the time he died as president three years later he had become a 32nd degree member and a Shriner. Truman served as Grand Master of the Missouri lodge.

Some idea of the prestige of Masonry may be gained by a brief survey of the caliber of men who have knocked at Masonry's doors. They include Benjamin Franklin (who helped initiate Voltaire into the lodge), Paul Revere, Alexander Hamilton, Patrick Henry, Lafay-

---

[2] John Gunther, *Inside U.S.A.* (New York: Harper & Bros., 1947), p. 338.

ette, John Jacob Astor, Mark Twain, Henry Ford, Will Rogers, General Pershing, Henry Clay, John Philip Sousa, Bolivar, Sam Houston, Irving Berlin, Charles Lindbergh, and J. Edgar Hoover. We should note that Benedict Arnold and Aaron Burr were also Masons as were most of the leaders of the revived Ku Klux Klan.

Masonic orators and writers often assert that between forty and fifty of the 55 signers of the Declaration of Independence were Masons but the Masonic research scholar, Gen. John C. Smith of Chicago, found that only six signers could be identified as lodge members. Masonry experienced a decline from the Morgan incident until after the Civil War so that we find that neither Lincoln nor Grant, Jefferson Davis nor Lee were Masons.

All Masons belong to a local Blue Lodge just as all Catholics belong to a parish. In some Southern and Midwestern communities practically all white members of the middle class who are Protestant and 21 are nominal or active members of the lodge. A hard core of members usually supplies the lodge officers who must attend all meetings; *Time* magazine recently estimated that fewer than 15 per cent of the paid-up membership attend the regular meetings although more will turn out for a New Year's Eve dance or banquet.[3] Of the 16,000 Blue Lodges in the United States in 1957, 60 use a foreign language in the ritual and business meetings and half of these are German lodges.

Blue Lodges in each state of the union and the District of Columbia are grouped in Grand Lodges directed by Grand Masters. In most countries these Grand Lodges are national bodies but all attempts to form such a nationwide Grand Lodge of the United States have failed. At one time Washington was proposed as Grand Master but this plan fell through and was shelved indefinitely after his death. In 1798 the first president wrote: "The fact is, I preside over none (lodge); nor have I been in one more than once or twice within the last thirty years." We can excuse Masonic enthusiasts who are tempted to exaggerate the role of the lodge in the lives of such patriots as Washington and Franklin. The latter never bothered to mention Masonry in his famous *Autobiography*.

---

[3] *Time*, August 26, 1957, p. 18.

THE MASONIC STRUCTURE

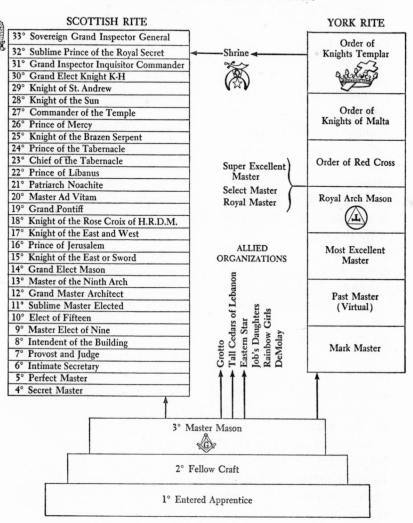

SCOTTISH RITE	YORK RITE
33° Sovereign Grand Inspector General	Order of Knights Templar
32° Sublime Prince of the Royal Secret	
31° Grand Inspector Inquisitor Commander	
30° Grand Elect Knight K-H	
29° Knight of St. Andrew	Order of Knights of Malta
28° Knight of the Sun	
27° Commander of the Temple	
26° Prince of Mercy	
25° Knight of the Brazen Serpent	
24° Prince of the Tabernacle	Order of Red Cross
23° Chief of the Tabernacle	
22° Prince of Libanus	
21° Patriarch Noachite	Royal Arch Mason
20° Master Ad Vitam	
19° Grand Pontiff	
18° Knight of the Rose Croix of H.R.D.M.	
17° Knight of the East and West	
16° Prince of Jerusalem	Most Excellent Master
15° Knight of the East or Sword	
14° Grand Elect Mason	
13° Master of the Ninth Arch	
12° Grand Master Architect	Past Master (Virtual)
11° Sublime Master Elected	
10° Elect of Fifteen	
9° Master Elect of Nine	
8° Intendent of the Building	Mark Master
7° Provost and Judge	
6° Intimate Secretary	
5° Perfect Master	
4° Secret Master	

Shrine

Super Excellent Master
Select Master
Royal Master

ALLIED ORGANIZATIONS

Grotto
Tall Cedars of Lebanon
Eastern Star
Job's Daughters
Rainbow Girls
DeMolay

3° Master Mason

2° Fellow Craft

1° Entered Apprentice

Many Masons are thoroughly bored by the routine of the Blue Lodge meetings and by its insipid initiations but are led on like a rabbit after a carrot to enter the "higher degrees." They can advance in the Masonic hierarchy by one or both of two main routes as their spare time and pocketbook dictate: the Scottish and York rites. The former consists of 30 degrees superimposed on the basic three and topped by the honorary 33rd degree; the York rite leads to membership in the Knights Templar. Knights Templar and 32nd degree Masons are eligible for entry into the Shrine.

Masonry was transplanted to these shores from England less than a decade after the founding of the first Grand Lodge in 1717. Franklin became a member in 1731 and rose rapidly in Masonic ranks. Perhaps a majority of the colonial leaders in the Revolutionary War were Masons. A part in the Boston Tea Party is claimed by some Masonic writers since the records indicate that the Lodge of St. Andrew adjourned early for lack of members in attendance and the Minute Book is inscribed with a large "T."

By the end of the War Masonic lodges were flourishing in the colonies and enjoyed the prestige of Washington and other national heroes who had been Masons. But Masonic growth was abruptly halted by the Morgan incident in 1826.

A 38-foot monument in Batavia, New York, has been erected to the memory of Morgan. The inscription at the foot of the monument reads: "Sacred to the memory of Wm. Morgan, a native of Virginia, a captain in the War of 1812, a respectable citizen of Batavia, and a martyr to the freedom of writing, printing and speaking the truth. He was abducted from near this spot in the year 1826, by Freemasons, and murdered for revealing the secrets of their order."

Morgan, a disillusioned Mason, had written an exposé of the lodge which so angered the Masons in the vicinity that they kidnaped the author and took him to Fort Niagara. He was never again seen alive but a body was later identified as his and the general public concluded that for once Masons had taken their obligation to protect their secrets and punish offenders in a serious rather than a symbolic sense. Three men were eventually given prison terms for their part in the affair while Masons have insisted that Morgan simply escaped and became a missing rather than a murdered person. Some say he ended up as a Moslem.

As a result of this scandal, an anti-Masonic party was formed which polled 128,000 votes in the 1830 election and carried Vermont in the campaign against Jackson in 1832. Rhode Island and Vermont passed laws against the oaths demanded by secret societies. Thousands who had joined the lodge for business and political advantage burned their aprons. Membership in the New York lodges dropped from 30,000 to 300 in a few years time. Associations of Protestant churches denounced all secret societies, hundreds of lodges dissolved, and 130 anti-Masonic periodicals began publication as a direct result of the Morgan incident. It is only just to say that evidence that irate Masons actually murdered Morgan is inconclusive although the fact of the kidnaping itself has been established.

Meanwhile the Independent Order of Odd Fellows offered the mysteries of a secret ritual and certain insurance benefits to the workingman and the farmer. The Knights of Pythias, an American invention, was established by a group of government clerks in 1864. Both were forbidden by the Church in 1894 but such affiliation did not entail excommunication as in the case of Masonry and under certain conditions Catholics may retain nominal membership in these two orders. The Grand Army of the Republic and the National Grange and other semisecret societies were founded by Masons along Masonic principles.

By the turn of the century the Morgan affair was almost forgotten and Masonry had ingratiated itself with large sections of Protestantism. It resumed its advance into a position of preeminence among American secret societies.

Some sociologists attribute the spectacular growth of the lodge in this country to the barrenness of Puritan worship and the absence of royalty and its attendant ceremonials. Some say that the matriarchal influences in American society drive the men into Masonic lodges where they can bar all women, exchange secret passwords, assume outlandish titles, and participate in manly rites. The current vogue of conformity which has added millions to church rolls has also brought thousands to the doors of the temple since Masonic initiation appears to be "the thing to do." Masonry supplies the ritual, vestments, and mystery for American Methodists and Baptists which the Catholic Church offers through her ancient liturgy.

American Freemasonry is Jim Crow. Not only do Masons deny the legitimacy of Negro Masonic lodges but they refuse to initiate colored men into white lodges. The Grand Lodge of England authorized a lodge of Negroes in Boston which eventually assumed Grand Lodge status itself and chartered other Prince Hall lodges for men of color. The American Masonic authority Albert Pike declared in 1875: "Prince Hall lodge was as regular a Lodge as any Lodge created by competent authority. It had a perfect right to establish other lodges and make itself a Mother Lodge." Nevertheless white Masonry has never recognized this right and brands all Negro lodges as "clandestine." Negroes may not enter or visit a white lodge or even converse on Masonic subjects with white men. Today about 312,000 Negroes belong to Prince Hall lodges while thousands of others belong to bogus lodges. Parallel Negro bodies of the Scottish rite, Knights Templar, and Shrine have also been founded because the white bodies refused to admit nonwhites.

Pike declared in 1868: "Freemasonry is one faith, one great religion, one great common star around which men of all tongues and languages shall assemble." Nevertheless he declared, "I took my obligation to white men, not Negroes. When I have to accept Negroes as brethren or leave Masonry, I shall leave it." So much for Pike's conception of Masonic brotherhood.

When the Grand Lodge of Washington agreed to extend a partial recognition to Negro Masons in that state, every Grand Lodge in the United States and Canada severed fraternal relations with the Washington Grand Lodge. Masonry's attitude toward Negro Americans exposes the Craft's shallow ideas of the brotherhood of man under the fatherhood of God. The lodges reinforce the pattern of racial segregation in this country, particularly in the South where Masonry might have become a progressive force in this critical area. What is dismaying is that by 1961 not a single lodge in any of the 50 Grand Lodges, North or South, has had the courage to open its doors to Negroes.[4]

In an article on Prince Hall lodges the Negro picture magazine *Ebony* commented: "Like many other chinks in American democracy, Masonry in the U. S. today has not lived entirely up to its creed. While Prince Hall Masons are indisputedly legitimate by virtue of their original charter, their white brethren have been reluctant to extend a hand of fellowship. This, in spite of their fraternal teachings of brotherly love and the fact that they all pay homage to a biblical black man, King Solomon."[5]

In these prosperous times the American lodges find thousands of prospective members seeking admittance. The rival Knights of Pythias has all but faded out of the fraternal picture and the IOOF no longer attracts new blood. Television, the automobile, and the country club have cut deeply into lodge attendance and many members are Masons simply in virtue of the fact that they were initiated 20 or 30 years ago and have continued to send in their dues. A depression such as that of the 1930's would, in all probability, find hundreds of thousands of Masons dropping their lodge membership as one of the first luxuries to be eliminated. At the close of the relatively prosperous fiscal year which ended July 31, 1956, the Grand Lodge of California reported that 1,622 members withdrew from the Order and 980 were suspended for nonpayment of dues. Nevertheless, the California Grand Lodge could afford to dedicate a 6 million dollar Masonic Memorial Temple on Nob Hill in San Francisco in 1958.

Masonic benevolence is impressive only if we fail to examine the nature of this benevolence and the manner in which funds are collected. Unlike the Christian Church which admits young and old, rich and poor, male and female, sick and healthy, white and Negro, the lodge selects only those who are unlikely to need any assistance and who are able to contribute generously from their

---

[4] One of the 50 state Grand Lodges, that of New Jersey, provides token recognition of racial equality by admitting the legitimacy of Alpha Lodge No. 116, a Negro Masonic lodge in Newark.

[5] *Ebony*, September, 1958, p. 28.

surplus. Their charity is not that of the widow's mite but of the widow's son's surplus. In 1948 *Time* magazine estimated Masonic charity for the year at $9,000,000 which amounted to about $3 per capita. Through such assessments the order supported 4500 aged Masons and their wives in 30 homes and about 1500 orphaned and dependent children. Masonic benevolence is generally directed for the benefit of Masons in good standing rather than for the general poor and needy. In fact, this implied guarantee of assistance is one of the chief selling points of the lodge. The individual Mason, however, has no *quid pro quo* share in such assistance since the Masonic lodge does not operate an insurance program such as that of the Knights of Columbus. The Shrine, which does not constitute an integral part of Masonry, admits children of all creeds and color to its chain of orthopedic hospitals. Girard College is usually claimed as a Masonic benevolence and it is instructive to note that Girard's will stipulated that no Negroes and no clergymen were ever to set foot on the campus.

The Masonic lodges in the United States enroll some of the finest gentlemen in the nation. We will try to show that a person cannot be an intelligent Christian and an intelligent Mason but we will never question the sincerity of anyone who claims to be both; we must question his consistency in giving allegiance to an exclusive religion such as Christianity and to the religion of naturalism propagated by the Masonic lodge. For many Masons the influence of the lodge in their lives is slight; we have no way of measuring their degree of commitment to Masonic principles compared to their commitment to Jesus Christ. Certainly many "Christian Masons" display far more Christianity than Masonry in their daily lives.

CHAPTER II

ORIGIN OF MASONRY

King Solomon's Temple or an English Tavern?

Masonry as we know it dates from 1717 but Masonic legends claim a much greater antiquity for the Craft. Many naïve and credulous members take these fanciful pretensions seriously and believe that Masonry can be traced back to King Solomon's Temple or to the Tower of Babel. One discredited Masonic historian, Oliver, maintained that the lodge began with creation itself and that Adam was not only the first man but the first Masonic Grand Master. According to Oliver this pure Masonry became corrupted at the time of the Tower of Babel but was rediscovered and purified by St. John the Evangelist.

A candid appraisal of these fables is given by Durrah in his *History and Evolution of Freemasonry:* "Masons have believed the things concerning the origin of the institution that they wanted to believe and have gone forth and told them as facts. When links were missing, they have been supplied by drawing upon fertile imaginations."[1]

He adds: "If there is in Freemasonry any similarity between its customs and those of the practices of several thousand years ago, it does not mean that Freemasonry has any connection whatsoever with those rites but that they were woven into the fraternity in

---

[1] Delmar Duane Durrah, *History and Evolution of Freemasonry* (Chicago: Charles T. Powner Co., 1952), pp. 25–26.

13

modern times with a view to enhancing the ritual and investing the fraternity with an atmosphere of antiquity."[2]

We find the same attempt to gain prestige and posthumous patrons in a cult such as Jehovah's Witnesses. Adopting this name in 1931, the Witnesses now point to every Old Testament figure who is hailed as a witness (of Jehovah) and claimed as a pioneer member of the cult. Masons are led to believe by their ritual and various commentaries that King Solomon, Hiram of Tyre, Hiram Abiff, and St. John the Evangelist were all active members of the lodge. Intelligent Masons, of course, know this for the spoof that it is but many others never question the basic fraud behind the claim to antiquity. Their brethren, realizing the value of antiquity to *esprit de corps*, do not bother to disenchant them.

Modern Masonry has borrowed from many diverse traditions such as those of the suppressed Knights Templar, the Roman Collegia of Artificers, the Jewish Kabbalists, the mystery cults, the Rosicrucians, and the operative masons of the Middle Ages. The Masonic historians Pick and Knight admit:

> Many of the doctrines or tenets inculcated in Freemasonry belong to the vast traditions of humanity of all ages and all parts of the world. Nevertheless, not only has no convincing evidence yet been brought forward to prove the lineal descent of our Craft from any ancient organization which is known to have, or even suspected of having, taught any similar system of morality, but also from what we know of the Craft in the few centuries prior to the formation of the first Grand Lodge in 1717, it is excessively unlikely that there was any such parentage.[3]

Of the various influences which contributed to the Masonic fraternity the greatest was that of the working masons. Fr. Humphrey J. T. Johnston states: "Modern Freemasonry, the creation of Deists and Jews with a measure of Huguenot assistance, built on a foundation provided by the old confraternities of stonemasons which in a degenerate form had survived the Reformation."[4]

---

[2] *Ibid.*, p. 36.
[3] Pick and Knight, *The Pocket History of Freemasonry* (New York: Philosophical Library, 1953), p. 9.
[4] Humphrey J. T. Johnston, *Freemasonry, a Short Historical Sketch* (London: Catholic Truth Society, 1952), p. 3.

These working masons who built the magnificent cathedrals and castles of medieval Europe and were greatly esteemed for their "know how," served as apprentices and fellow craftsmen before qualifying as master masons. They devised a system of secret signs and grips which served the purpose of today's union card and identified the initiated as properly qualified workmen. Masons were forced to travel from place to place to pursue their occupation; membership in the powerful stonemasons' guild meant that a mason could rely on help from his brethren in difficult circumstances and in strange lands. He could likewise be counted upon to preserve trade secrets from outsiders.

After the Reformation had practically halted the construction of new church buildings the waning masonic lodges began to admit "honorary" or nonworking members to their ranks. The original lodges were unquestionably orthodox in their adherence to the Catholic religion which they served so admirably. One of the earliest masonic charges reads: "The first charge is that you shall bee true man to God and holy church, and that you use no heresie or error by your understanding or by teachings of indiscreet men."

Eventually the honorary members outnumbered the operative masons, more or less dispossessed the actives, and took over the symbols and secret signs of the lodges to form what we know as speculative Masonry. Members were expected to believe in God and in the immortality of the soul but otherwise their religious views were completely irrelevant to the lodge.

In 1717 a governing authority known as the "Grand Lodge of England" was established at a meeting of four surviving lodges in the Apple Tree tavern in London. Two Protestant clergymen, Dr. John Theosophilus Desaguliers and Dr. James Anderson, were instrumental in setting up the self-styled governing body. Not all lodges were willing to submit to the rule of the new Grand Lodge but by 1725 the original four lodges had grown to 64 of which 50 were in London. The Craft captured the fancy of certain members of the English aristocracy after 1721 and they in turn were flattered by the brethren. The first royal Grand Master took office in that year and this position has since been reserved to a nobleman.

Originally some lodges worked one degree and others, two. The Hiramic legend which forms the basis for the present Master Mason degree was introduced by Anderson sometime after 1720 and the three-degree system was not adopted until 1730.

Anderson prepared a new *Book of Constitutions* in 1723 which spelled out the new policy of the lodge toward religious affiliation. "A Mason is obliged by his Tenure, to obey the Moral Law, and if he rightly understand the Art, he will never be a stupid Atheist nor an irreligious Libertine. But though in ancient times Masons were charged in every country to be of the Religion of that Country or Nation, whatever it was, yet 'tis now thought more expedient only to oblige them to that Religion in which all Men agree, leaving their particular opinions to themselves that is, to be good Men and true, or Men of Honour and Honesty, by whatsoever Denominations or Persuasions they may be distinguished. . . ."

Obviously the religion to which Masons in ancient times were expected to adhere was Catholicism since it was the religion of Europe. Obviously, too, the "Religion in which all Men agree" is not Catholicism or Christianity since many men do not agree with the central theological positions of Christianity. These central beliefs are relegated to the role of "particular opinions."

This change in policy opened the door to membership by Jews, Deists, and Moslems but supposedly barred atheists and polytheists. Jews might well feel at home in the lodge since the Hiram Abiff legend was built on the Old rather than the New Testament and the Craft borrowed most of its terminology from the Hebrew. The core of Masonry, that mankind has suffered a great loss which eventually will be recovered, could easily be understood to mean the loss of the Temple and of Jewish nationhood.

Although the aristocrats took up the Masonic hobby, the lower classes often sneered at the Masonic falderal and snob appeal and enjoyed pelting participants in Masonic processions. The lodges continued to meet in taverns and were known as convivial associations. The first published exposés began to appear.

Eventually a rival Grand Lodge was founded which charged that the main body had de-Christianized the Craft (which it had), had transposed the modes of recognition in the first and second degrees, omitted certain prayers, ignored Saints' days, and committed other crimes. The dissidents took the name "Antients" and labeled the original Grand Lodge the "Moderns." The rivalry continued from 1751 to 1813 when two royal brothers headed the opposing factions and agreed to sign the articles of reunion. The amalgamated Grand Lodge agreed to include the Royal Arch degree favored by the Antients as a part of pure and ancient Masonry although most Masons in England as in America never take this degree. The Antients completed the Masonic apostasy by compromising on every point in which they had claimed to uphold the Christian orientation of the Craft. Reunion of the Antients and Moderns in America followed the English reunion by four years.

From England the Craft spread to the continent and to British colonies throughout the world, often serving as a handy instrument of British policy. Although the Church's basic objections to Masonry apply to all branches of the Craft, we can distinguish two main Masonic traditions: those of Anglo-Saxon Masonry including England, Scotland, the United States, Holland, and the Scandinavian countries, and those of the Grand Orients such as France, Spain, Italy, and South America. We shall review the status of Latin and European Masonry in Chapter X. Suffice to say, the attitude of the Church toward the lodge meant that in Catholic nations only religious rebels and Jews sought admission to the lodges. This concentration of atheists, agnostics, freethinkers, Jews, and anticlericals turned Latin Masonry into a subversive and hostile critic of Christianity and all religions. When the Grand Orient of France in 1877 rejected the landmark of belief in God and removed the Bible from the lodges, the Anglo-Saxons severed fraternal relations which have never been resumed.

Latin Freemasonry grew increasingly revolutionary and anticlerical after 1860 but seems to be undergoing a process of disintegration today. English Freemasonry went on to become ultrarespectable, bourgeois, vaguely Protestant, royalist, and white supremist. In the

United States as well as in England the lodge has assumed the proportions of a mass movement among the white Protestant middle class rather than an elite. The Catholic heritage of the operative Masonic lodges has been all but obliterated and the brethren have long been nourished on a concoction of fables and falsehoods regarding the origin of the fraternity.

CHAPTER III

MASONIC INITIATION

Three Degrees Comprise the Blue Lodge

Candidates for the Masonic Order must receive a series of three degrees before reaching full membership in the Blue Lodge; these are the basic degrees for all other Masonic honors. They are "entered" as Entered Apprentices, "passed" as Fellow Crafts, and "raised" as Master Masons in ceremonies on three separate evenings or occasions of meeting. Once Master Masons, they supposedly know all Masonic secrets which will enable them to "travel and work in foreign countries and receive wages as such."

Each candidate petitions in writing for admittance and must be recommended by two members. Strictly speaking, he may not be prompted or solicited by Masonic friends or relatives. Actually, although the lodge abstains from membership campaigns and similar hoopla, most prospective members are sold on the advantages of affiliation by some other Mason. The writer has talked to Protestant ministers who revealed that they had been importuned several times in their careers to enter the lodge but, for religious reasons, regularly declined the invitations.

A duly assembled Masonic lodge consists of at least seven Freemasons acting under a charter or dispensation from some Grand Lodge. They assemble in a lodge room on the second or third floor of a building well guarded against "cowans" (a Masonic term for eavesdroppers) and the non-Masonic "profane." When

19

the candidate petitions for membership and submits his initiation fee of from $20 to $200, the Worshipful Master upon hearing the application read in meeting, appoints an Investigating Committee of three Blue Lodge Masons to investigate the character of the applicant and to report at the next regular meeting. Favorable recommendations from at least two of the Investigating Committee are sufficient to bring the application to vote. If on the first ballot all balls are white (or "clear"), the candidate is declared elected to receive the degrees. If one black appears, the ballot is "cloudy" and it is necessary to vote a second time; and, if on the second ballot a black ball appears, the candidate is rejected. Of course, two black balls on the first ballot also means rejection. A unanimous vote is required.

On the appointed night for conferring the First or Entered Apprentice Degree, the local lodge conducts a Lodge of Entered Apprentices. The usual officers include Worshipful Master, Senior Warden, Junior Warden, Secretary, Treasurer, Senior Deacon, Junior Deacon, Senior and Junior Stewards and the Tyler (doorkeeper). The latter is usually an elderly gentleman who may receive a few dollars for tending the door. The Secretary may also be a paid officer.

Before presenting the working of the degrees, we should explain that the ritual as presented in this chapter is that used in most American lodges. There may be trivial verbal variations but no printed ritual could possibly conform to all the various rituals in use by the 49 Grand Lodges in this country. An analogy might be found in translations of the Lord's Prayer. One Christian body uses "which" and another "who art in heaven," one uses "debts" and "debtor" and another, "trespasses" and "those who tresspass against us," and some add the ending "for thine is the kingdom and the power and the glory forever," which most Christians consider a liturgical interpolation. Nevertheless, we know that we have the substance of the Our Father.

The reader should remember that his Masonic friends have taken an oath to conceal this ritual and will either refuse to discuss it altogether, change the subject, or simply deny its authenticity.

Masonic candidate prepared to
receive the first or
Entered Apprentice degree.

Unless a Mason is well traveled and informed, he may honestly believe that since the work in his lodge differs slightly from that given in this chapter, this printed ritual is defective. If he has visited lodges in other states and has studied other rituals he will know that minor differences exist in all of the 49 Grand Lodge rituals.

Three reasons account for the variations in rituals among the dozens of Masonic jurisdictions. First, there has never been a uniform ritual in England, the birthplace of the craft, and therefore the American lodges inherited not one, but several rituals. Second, until the beginning of the past century English and American Masons considered it unessential to commit the ritual to memory in the word for word memorization which is now demanded. Third, the two rival English lodges, "Antients" and "Moderns" developed their own rituals and delivered these to their American counterparts. Masonic research workers can find predominantly Modern workings in Rhode Island, North Carolina, and Ohio, and Antient workings in New York, New Jersey, and Michigan.

Each Grand Lodge employs a Grand Lecturer who travels about the state giving instruction in the rituals and is supported by stipends from the lodges he visits. The material in this chapter has been gathered from decodings of the published *Ecce Orienti* (sometimes referred to as *King Solomon's*) books which are used by lodge officers. Each state has its own version and the code employed can be broken by elementary cryptography. Two printed rituals, Ronayne and Duncan, are substantially accurate and often used by Masons themselves who do not wish to bother with the coded books. The details of the ritual are corroborated by Masonic Monitors, catalogs of paraphernalia, references in Masonic texts, and the testimony of seceders. The material in this chapter has been checked by three former Masons, including a Worshipful Master and two 32nd Degree Masons, who are now active Catholic laymen. Any large Catholic parish is likely to have one or more Masons who have renounced the lodge and joined the Church. The idea of genuine secrets in a mass organization of 4,000,000 men in the United States alone is preposterous and we would not labor the point except that many seem to think that Masonry manages to keep its initiations and lodge rituals from those non-Masons who are interested in knowing them.

To keep this chapter within bounds, we have eliminated unnecessary repetitions and details which would serve no real purpose. A verbatim account of the ritual and rubrics would comprise a small book in itself.

The interior of the lodge room features an altar in the center on which rests a Bible and the Square and Compass. Nearby are three lighted tapers. The letter "G" is suspended or painted over the Master's chair and may be interpreted to stand for geometry

EAST

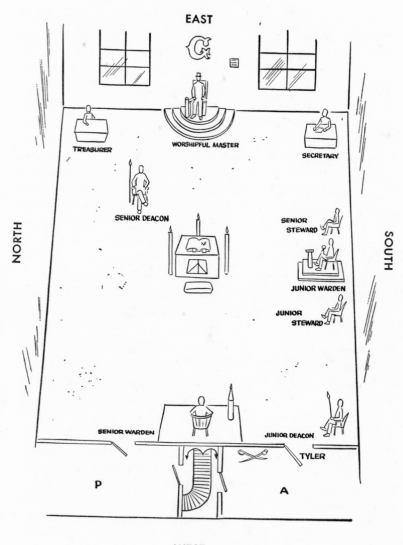

NORTH

SOUTH

WEST

Floor plan of Masonic lodge indicating position of officers

or God.[1] The Worshipful Master sits in the east and wears his apron, hat, sash, and jewel of office. Other members wear their white aprons and jewels of office if officeholders.

If candidates are to be inducted as Entered Apprentices, the Master calls the lodge to order in that degree. He begins, "I now declare this Lodge of Master Masons closed and Entered Apprentice in its stead. Brother Junior Deacon, inform the Tyler (the door-keeper); Brother Senior Deacon, attend at the altar (place both points of the compass under the square)." He raps once and the members take their seats. He then instructs the Junior Deacon to take his assistants (Senior Steward and Junior Steward) to the anteroom where the candidate is waiting.

The Secretary accompanies them to the anteroom and obtains affirmative answers to the following questions:

"Do you seriously declare, upon your honor, that, unbiased by friends, and uninfluenced by mercenary motives, you freely and voluntarily offer yourself a candidate for the mysteries of Masonry?"

"Do you seriously declare, upon your honor, that you are prompted to solicit the privileges of Masonry by a favorable opinion of the institution, a desire for knowledge, and a sincere wish of being of service to your fellow creatures?"

"Do you seriously declare, upon your honor, that you will conform to all the ancient established usages of the Order?"

The Secretary returns to the lodge room and reports that the candidate has given the required answers. The candidate is now prepared for the first degree. He is instructed to remove his coat, shoes and stockings, and trousers and is divested of all metal articles: coins, watch, rings, etc.[2] The Junior Deacon gives him a pair of trousers furnished by the lodge and asks him to put his left arm through the front of his shirt, exposing a bare arm and

---

[1] "The majority of masonic writers believe that the letter 'G' refers to Geometry, and the old catechisms also point that way." Bernard E. Jones, *Freemasons' Guide and Compendium* (London: George G. Harrap, 1950), p. 299.

[2] "Freemasonry is essentially a Solar Cult and this prejudice against the use of m . . . ls (metals) in connection with religious observances is nearly always associated with the worship of the benign Spirits of Light." J. S. M. Ward, *The Masonic Why and Wherefore* (London: Baskerville Press, 1929), p. 1.

left breast. The Deacon then puts a blindfold (called a hoodwink) on the candidate, places a slipper on his right foot and loops a blue silk rope, called a cabletow, around his neck.

He leads the hoodwinked candidate to the lodge door and gives three knocks. The Senior Deacon inside reports "Worshipful Master, there is an alarm at the inner door of our Lodge." The Master asks him to ascertain the cause of the alarm and the Junior Deacon speaking for the Candidate responds, "Mr. —— who has long been

Interior of a Masonic lodge facing Worshipful Master's station

in darkness, and now seeks to be brought to light, and to receive a part in the rights and benefits of this worshipful Lodge, erected to God, and dedicated to the holy Sts. John, as all brothers and fellows have done before."[3]

In a series of questions put to the Junior Deacon the Senior Deacon asks if the candidate is "worthy and well qualified," "duly and truly prepared," "of lawful age and properly vouched for," and "a man, free born, of good repute, and well recommended." The Senior Deacon closes the door, relays the answers to the Master, and takes the compass from the altar.

As the candidate and Junior Deacon enter the Lodge room, the Senior Deacon presses one of the points of the compass to the candidate's bare left breast. "Mr. ——, on entering this Lodge for the first time, I receive you on the point of a sharp instrument pressing your naked left breast, which is to teach you, as this is an instrument of torture to your flesh, so should the recollection of it ever be to your mind and conscience, should you attempt to reveal the secrets of Masonry unlawfully." This ceremony is known as the "Shock of Entrance" or "Rite of Induction."

The Senior Deacon now takes over from the Junior Deacon and guides the candidate around the room. The Master interrupts, however, by asking "Let no one enter on so important a duty without first invoking the blessing of the Deity. Brother Senior Deacon, you will conduct the candidate to the center of the Lodge, and cause him to kneel for the benefit of prayer." The Master leaves his seat and kneels next to the candidate at the Masonic altar. They repeat the following prayer:

---

[3] "Without question Masonry demands of its adherent a denial of the Christian (and of every other so-called sectarian) religion. He must come as one in darkness, seeking light from the lodge, as one who is in spiritual ignorance, seeking wisdom. Since the lodge is nothing if not religious . . . it is religious light, religious wisdom, which is promised to its candidates. And by declaring that they are in darkness, the applicants formally, though not always consciously, reject the religious teachings of their Church as darkness. There is no escape from the conclusion that Masonry promises all of its members that they will find a higher, better religion in the lodge than is offered by the Christian Church." Theodore Graebner, *Is Masonry a Religion?* (St. Louis: Concordia Publishing House, 1946), p. 24.

Vouchsafe Thine aid, Almighty Father of the Universe, to this our present convention; and grant that this candidate for Masonry may dedicate and devote his life to Thy service, and become a true and faithful brother among us! Endue him with a competency of Thy divine wisdom, that, by the secrets of our art, he may be better enabled to display the beauties of brotherly love, relief, and truth, to the honor of Thy Holy Name. Amen.

All respond with the Masonic "So mote it be."

The Master rises, replaces his top hat and takes the candidate by the right hand. "Mr. ——, in whom do you put your trust?" The candidate is prompted to answer, "In God." The Master comments, "Since in God you put your trust, your faith is well founded. Arise, follow your conductor and fear no danger." The candidate is then led around the lodge and the same questions put by the Senior Deacon earlier are repeated by the Junior Warden and Senior Warden. The Master also interrogates the candidate and continues, "From whence come you, and whither are you traveling?" The Senior Deacon answers for the candidate, "From the west, and traveling toward the east." Master: "Why leave you the west and travel toward the east?" Senior Deacon: "In search of light."

Master: "Since light is the object of your search, you will re-conduct the candidate, and place him in charge of the Senior Warden in the west, with my orders that he teach this candidate to approach the east, the place of light, by advancing with one upright, regular step to the first stop, the heel of his right placed in the hollow of his left foot, his body erect at the altar before the Worshipful Master in the east."

The Senior Warden sees that the candidate assumes the proper posture and tells the Master that he is ready. Again the Master leaves his seat and approaches the altar. "Mr. ——, you are now at the altar of Masonry for the first time, before you can be permitted to advance any further in Masonry, it becomes my duty to inform you, that you must take upon yourself a solemn oath or obligation, appertaining to this degree, which I, as Master of this Lodge, assure you will not materially interfere with the duty that you owe to your God, yourself, family, country, or neighbor. Are you willing to take such an oath?"

He replies that he is willing and the Master continues, "Brother Senior Warden, you will place the candidate in due form, which is by kneeling on his naked left knee, his right forming the angle of a square, his left hand supporting the Holy Bible, square and compass, his right hand resting thereon. Mr. ——, you are now in position for taking upon yourself the solemn oath of an Entered Apprentice Mason, and, if you have no objections still, you will say I, and repeat your name after me."

"I, ——, of my own free will and accord, in the presence of Almighty God, and this Worshipful Lodge, erected to Him, and dedicated to the holy Sts. John, do hereby and hereon (Master presses his gavel on candidate's knuckles) most solemnly and sincerely promise and swear, that I will always hail, ever conceal, and never reveal any of the arts, parts, or points of the hidden mysteries of Ancient Free Masonry, which may have been, or hereafter shall be, at this time, or any future period, communicated to me, as such, to any person or persons whomsoever, except it be to a true and lawful brother Mason, or in a regularly constituted Lodge of Masons; nor unto him or them until, by strict trial, due examination, or lawful information, I shall have found him, or them, as lawfully entitled to the same as I am myself. I furthermore promise and swear that I will not print, paint, stamp, stain, cut, carve, mark or engrave them, or cause the same to be done, on any thing movable or immovable, capable of receiving the least impression of a word, syllable, letter, or character, whereby the same may become legible or intelligible to any person under the canopy of heaven, and the secrets of Masonry thereby unlawfully obtained through my unworthiness.

"All this I most solemnly, sincerely promise and swear, with a firm and steadfast resolution to perform the same, without any mental reservation or secret evasion of mind whatever, binding myself under no less penalty than that of having my throat cut across, my tongue torn out by its roots, and my body buried in the rough sands of the sea, at low-water mark, where the tide ebbs and flows twice in twenty-four hours, should I ever knowingly violate this my Entered Apprentice obligation. So help me God, and keep me steadfast in the due performance of the same."

At the end of the oath the Master asks, "In token of your sincerity you will now detach your hands, and kiss the book on which your hands rest, which is the Holy Bible." The candidate complies and the Master tells the Senior Deacon to release the cable tow since "he is bound to us by an obligation — a tie stronger than lower hands can impose," and is again asked what he most desires. He is prompted to say "Light." At this the Master says, "Brethren you will stretch forth your hands, and assist me in bringing our newly made brother to light." The brethren surrounding the altar place their hands in the form of the Entered Apprentice duegard and the Master quotes from Genesis, "In the beginning God created the heavens and the earth. And the earth was without form, and void; and darkness was upon the face of the waters. And God said, Let there be light, and there was light." At this the conductor jerks the blindfold from the candidate's eyes and he sees the assembled lodge for the first time.

The Master now explains the lights of Masonry. "My brother, on being brought to light in this degree, you discover both points of the compass hid by the square, which is to signify that you are yet in darkness as respects Masonry, you having only received the degree of an Entered Apprentice. You also discover the three great lights of Masonry, by the help of the three lesser. The three great lights in Masonry are the Holy Bible, square, and compass, which are thus explained: the Holy Bible is the rule and guide of our faith and practice; the square our actions; the compass, to circumscribe and keep us within bounds with all mankind, but more especially with a brother Mason. The three lesser lights are the three burning tapers which you see placed in a triangular form about this altar. They represent the sun, moon, and Master of the Lodge; and as the sun rules the day, and the moon governs the night, so ought the Worshipful Master to endeavor to rule and govern his Lodge with equal regularity."

Now the Master reveals the secret grip of this degree which con-

Duegard of an Entered Apprentice

Sign of an Entered Apprentice

Duegard of a Fellow Craft Mason

Sign of a Fellow Craft Mason

Duegard of a Master Mason

Sign of a Master Mason

Grand hailing sign of distress

sists of pressing the thumb on the joint of the candidate's index finger. The Master and Senior Deacon then engage in a routine on the following order:

Master: What do you conceal?

Senior Deacon: All the secrets of Masons in Masonry to which this (here presses his thumb on the joint) token alludes.

Master: What is that?

S.D.: A grip.

Master: Of what?

S.D.: Of an Entered Apprentice Mason.

Master: Has it a name?

S.D.: It has.

Master: Will you give it me?

S.D.: I did not so receive it, neither will I so impart it.

Master: How will you dispose of it?

S.D.: I will letter and halve it with you.

Master: Letter and begin.

S.D.: No, you begin.

Master: You must begin.

S.D.: A.

Master: Z.

S.D.: Az.

Master: B.

S.D.: O.

Master: Bo.

S.D.: Boaz.

The candidate passes around the room, giving the duegard and sign of the Entered Apprentice at the various officers' stations. The Master presents a white lambskin apron to the candidate and says: "Brother, I now present you with a lambskin or white apron, which is an emblem of innocence and the badge of a Mason, more ancient than the Golden Fleece or Roman Eagle, and, when worthily worn, more honorable than the Star and Garter, or any other order that can be conferred on you at this time, or any future period, by kings, princes, and potentates, or any other persons, except it be by Masons. I trust that you will wear it with equal pleasure to yourself and honor to the fraternity. You will carry it to the Senior Warden in the west, who will teach you how to wear it as an Entered Apprentice." The Senior Warden ties it on the candidate with the flap turned up.

Now the Master addresses the candidate, "Brother ——, agreeably to an ancient custom, adopted among Masons, it is necessary that you should be requested to deposit something of a metallic kind or nature, not for its intrinsic value, but that it may be laid up among the relics in the archives of this Lodge, as a memento that you were herein made a Mason. Anything, brother, that you may have about you will be thankfully received — a coin, a pin, anything."

Since the candidate was stripped of all his metallic possessions in the anteroom prior to entering the lodge, he has nothing to contribute. His offer to get something from his coat or trousers is refused and he is usually somewhat embarrassed.

"Brother ——, you are indeed an object of charity — almost naked, not one cent, not even a button or pin to bestow on this Lodge. Let this ever have, my brother, a lasting effect on your mind and conscience; and remember, should you ever see a friend, but more especially a brother, in a like destitute condition, you will contribute as liberally to his support and relief as his necessities may seem to demand and your ability permit, without any material injury to yourself or family."

Now the candidate is allowed to return to the preparation room and get dressed. He puts on his apron and returns to the room where the Master may take the occasion to deliver a sermon on the glories of the Craft and the meaning of the working tools of the Entered Apprentice degree: the 24-inch gauge and the common gavel. The candidate is assigned to an older Mason who will instruct him in the lecture of the degrees, a sort of catechism which the candidate must memorize prior to receiving the next degree and repeat at a later meeting to a committee designated to test his proficiency. It recapitulates the details of the ritual. Finally the Master delivers the Charge:

"As you are now introduced into the first principles of Masonry, I congratulate you on being accepted into this ancient and honorable order; ancient, as having existed from time immemorial; and honorable, as tending in every particular so to render all men who will conform to its precepts. No human institution was ever raised on a better principle, or more solid foundation; nor were ever more excellent rules and useful maxims laid down than are inculcated in the several Masonic lectures. The greatest and best of men in all ages have been encouragers and promoters of the art, and have never deemed it derogatory to their dignity to level themselves with the fraternity, extend their privileges, and patronize their assemblies.

"There are three great duties, which, as a Mason, you are strictly to observe and inculcate — to God, your neighbor, and yourself. To God, in never mentioning His name but with that reverential awe which is due from a creature to his Creator: to implore His aid in all your laudable undertakings, and to esteem Him as your chief good. To your neighbor, in acting upon the square, and doing unto him as you would he should do unto you; and to yourself, in avoiding all irregularity and intemperance, which may impair your faculties or debase the dignity of your profession. A zealous attachment to these duties will insure public and private esteem.

"In the State you are to be a quiet and peaceable citizen, true to your government, and just to your country; you are not to countenance disloyalty or rebellion, but patiently submit to legal authority, and conform with cheerfulness to the government of the country in which you live.

"In your outward demeanor be particularly careful to avoid censure or reproach. Let not interest, favor, or prejudice bias your integrity, or influence you to be guilty of a dishonorable action. And although your frequent appearance at our regular meetings is earnestly solicited, yet it is not meant that Masonry should interfere with your necessary avocations, for these are on no account to be neglected; neither are you to suffer your zeal for the institution to lead you into arguments with those who, through ignorance, may ridicule it. But, at your leisure hours, that you may improve in Masonic knowledge, you are to converse with well informed brethren, who will be always as ready to give as you will be ready to receive instruction.

"Finally, keep sacred and inviolable the mysteries of the Order, as these are to distinguish you from the rest of the community, and mark your consequence among Masons. If, in the circle of your acquaintance, you find a person desirous of being initiated into Masonry, be particularly careful not to recommend him, unless you are convinced he will conform to our rules; that the honor, glory, and reputation of the institution may be firmly established, and the world at large convinced of its good effects."

The lodge is now closed and the candidate will return on a later evening to take the second degree, that of Fellow Craft.

Many lodges find that few members bother to turn out for the working of this second degree. The curiosity about the new members is satisfied and the substance of this degree is dull and commonplace.

The candidate is stripped of his clothing as in the preparation for the Entered Apprentice degree but this time he slips his right arm out of his shirtsleeve exposing his right arm and breast. The cable tow is wound twice around his arm and the right foot and knee is bared. He is blindfolded and a slipper is placed on his left foot. The Junior Deacon knocks on the lodge room door and answers the Senior Deacon's inquiry with "Brother ——, who has been regularly initiated as Entered Apprentice, and now wishes to receive more light in Masonry by being passed to the degree of Fellow Craft." He answers a short series of questions regarding the candidate's proficiency in the first degree. The Junior Deacon whispers the pass "Shibboleth" to the Senior Deacon who closes the door, reports to the Master, and repeats the interrogations.

This time the Senior Deacon takes the square rather than the compass from the altar, and opening the door, says, "Let him enter and be received in due form." He places the angle of the square against the candidate's bare breast and declares, "Brother ——, on entering this Lodge the first time you were received on the points of a compass; I now receive you on the angle of the square, which is to teach you that the square of virtue should be the rule and guide of your conscience in all future transactions with mankind."

As the candidate is led twice around the lodge room, the Master reads a passage from the Old Testament: Amos 8:7, 8. He is questioned by the Junior and Senior Wardens and the Master regarding his proficiency in the previous degree and he tells the Master that he is in search of more light. Again the Master instructs the Senior Warden to teach the candidate the proper way to approach the east, this time by "two upright regular steps, his feet forming an angle of a square." He then places the candidate in position for taking his second oath. He kneels on his naked right knee before the altar, making his left knee form a square. His left arm from the shoulder to the elbow is held in a horizontal position with his forearm in a vertical position, forming a square. His right hand rests on an open Bible. The Master once more assures the candidate that nothing in the oath will interfere with any obligation to God, family, country, neighbor, or self. The oath follows:

"I, —— of my own free will and accord, in the presence of Almighty God, and this Worshipful Lodge, erected to Him, and dedicated to the holy Sts. John, do hereby and hereon most solemnly and sincerely promise and swear that I will always hail, and ever conceal, and never reveal any of the secret arts, parts, or points of the Fellow Craft Degree to any person whomsoever, except it be to a true and lawful brother of this degree, or in a regularly constituted Lodge of Fellow Crafts; nor unto him or them until, by strict trial, due examination, or lawful information, I shall find him, or them, as lawfully entitled to the same as I am myself.

"I furthermore promise and swear that I will stand to, and abide by, all the laws, rules, and regulations of the Fellow Craft Degree, as far as the same shall come to my knowledge.

"Further, I will acknowledge and obey all due signs and summons sent to me from a Lodge of Fellow Crafts, or given me by a brother of that degree, if within the length of my cable-tow.

"Further, that I will aid and assist all poor, distressed, worthy Fellow Crafts, knowing them to be such, as far as their necessities may require, and my ability permit, without any injury to myself.

"Further, that I will not cheat, wrong, nor defraud a brother of this degree, knowingly, nor supplant him in any of his laudable undertakings.

"All this I most solemnly promise and swear with a firm and steadfast resolution to perform the same, without any hesitation, mental reservation, or self-evasion of mind whatever, binding myself under no less penalty than of having my breast torn open, my heart plucked out, and placed on the highest pinnacle of the temple there to be devoured by the vultures of the air, should I ever knowingly violate the Fellow Craft obligation. So help me God, and keep me steadfast in the due performance of the same."

The ritual closely follows that of the first degree: the candidate asks for more light, the hoodwink is removed, the Master instructs him in the grip and password. The pass grip of a Fellow Craft is "Shibboleth" while the name of the real grip is "Jachin" which is given letter by letter. The candidate, speaking through the conductor, now relays this information on pass and grips to the Junior and Senior Wardens. The latter tucks a corner of the Masonic apron under the string which is the manner in which Fellow Crafts must wear the emblem. The Master then explains the working tools of the degree: the plumb, square, and level.

Now the candidate is escorted out of the lodge room back to the anteroom and the lodge room is rearranged for his second entry. Two large pillars about 7 feet high are placed five feet apart near the door. Fifteen painted boards are arranged to represent three, five, and seven steps. The conductor addresses the candidate: "Brother ——, we are now about to make an ascent through a porch, by a flight of winding stairs, consisting of three, five, and seven steps, to a place representing the Middle Chamber of King Solomon's Temple, there to receive instructions relative to the wages due, and jewels of a Fellow Craft."

The conductor delivers a short commentary on Operative and Speculative Masonry. He reveals that the name of the left hand pillar is Boaz and that on the right, Jachin. They are supposed to represent the two pillars erected at the outer porch of King Solomon's Temple.

The first three steps have at least three meanings: the three principal stages of human life, namely, youth, manhood, and old age; also the "three principal supports in Masonry," Wisdom, Strength, and Beauty; and finally the three principal lodge officers, Master and Senior and Junior Wardens.

The five steps have two meanings: five orders of architecture (Tuscan, Doric, Ionic, Corinthian, and Composite) and five senses. The seven refer to all sorts of combinations: seven Sabbatical years, seven years building the temple, seven wonders of the world, seven planets, seven liberal arts and sciences. Take your choice.

Completing these 15 steps the Junior Warden asks the Senior Deacon to explain the pass "Shibboleth." He elaborates: "In consequence of a quarrel which long existed between Jephthah, judge of Israel, and the Ephraimites: the latter had been a stubborn rebellious people, whom Jephthah had endeavored to subdue by lenient measures, but to no effect. The Ephraimites, being highly incensed for not being called to fight and share in the rich spoils of the Ammonitish war, assembled a mighty army, and passed over the river Jordan to give Jephthah battle; but he, being apprised of their approach, called together the men of Gilead, and gave them battle, and put them to flight; and, to make his victory more complete, he ordered guards to be placed on the different passes on the banks of the river Jordan, and commanded, if the Ephraimites passed that way, Say ye Shibboleth; but they, being of a different tribe, could not frame to pronounce it aright, and pronounced it Sibboleth; which trifling defect proved them to be spies, and cost them their lives; and there fell at that time, at the different passes on the banks of the river Jordan, forty and two thousand. This word was also used by our ancient brethren to distinguish a friend from a foe, and has since been adopted as a password, to be given before entering every regulated and well-governed Lodge of Fellow Crafts."

Then the Senior Deacon asks for the real pass "Jachin" and they pass to the Master who delivers the following homily:

"The first thing that particularly attracted your attention on your passage here, was a representation of two brazen pillars, one on the left hand and the other on the right, which was explained to you by your conductor; after passing the pillars you passed a flight of winding stairs, consisting of three, five, and seven steps, which was likewise explained to you; after passing the stairs, you arrived at the outer door of the Middle Chamber, which you found closely guarded by the Junior Warden, who demanded of you the pass and token of the pass of a Fellow Craft; you next arrived at the inner door of the Middle Chamber, which you found guarded by the Senior Warden, who demanded of you the grip and word of a Fellow Craft. You have now arrived at the Middle Chamber where you are received and recorded a Fellow Craft. You are now entitled to wages, as such; which are, the Corn of nourishment, the Wine of refreshment, and the Oil of joy, which denote peace, harmony, and strength. You are also entitled to the jewels of Fellow Craft; which are, an attentive ear, an instructive tongue, and faithful breast. The attentive ear receives the sound from the instructive tongue, and the mysteries of Masonry are safely lodged in the repositor of faithful breasts."

He concludes with the charge and the candidate is left to memorize the lecture which rehashes the degree work.

At last the Masonic candidate is ready for the concluding degree, the third. As many as three candidates for the third degree will be inducted in one evening. All will go through the first section of the work together but then each candidate must complete the degree in a separate ceremony which lasts from an hour to an hour and a half. A medium-sized lodge which enrolls perhaps 30 new members a year will thus have to schedule at least ten Master Mason initiations.

This degree, built around the legend of the assassination of Hiram Abiff, the builder of King Solomon's Temple, sometimes takes up to two hours for its full performance. Nowhere in the Bible do we read anything about Hiram's tragic death; only Masonic myth fills in the details of his demise. During the conferring of this degree the lodge is known as the "Sanctum Sanctorum of King Solomon's Temple."

This time the candidate rolls up his trousers on both legs and takes both arms out of his shirt, leaving legs and breast bare. The silk cable tow is wrapped around his waist three times and he is blindfolded. He gains entry into the lodge room by answering the usual questions through his spokesman, the Junior Deacon, and gives the password, "Tubal Cain."

The Senior Deacon stops him at the door: "Brother ——, on entering this Lodge the first time, you were received on the point of the compass, pressing your naked left breast, the moral of which was explained to you. On entering the second time, you were received on the angle of the square, which was also explained to you. I now receive you on both points of the compass, extending from your naked left to your naked right breast, which is to teach you that as the vital parts of man are contained within the breast, so the most excellent tenets of our institution are contained between the points of the compass — which are Friendship, Morality, and Brotherly Love."

The Senior Deacon escorts the third degree candidate around the lodge room three times while the Master recites a passage from the Bible. Sometimes in larger lodges a musical paraphrase will be sung and accompanied on the organ. He is instructed by the Senior Warden to place his feet, heels touching and toes pointed outward. The Master then asks that the candidate kneel at the altar with both hands on the Bible, square, and compass. The Master Mason's oath follows:

"I, ——, of my own free will and accord, in the presence of Almighty God, and this Worshipful Lodge, erected to Him and dedicated to the holy Sts. John, do hereby and hereon most solemnly and sincerely promise and swear, that I will always hail, ever conceal, and never reveal any of the secrets, arts, parts, point or points, of the Master Masons' Degree, to any person or persons whomsoever, except that it be to a true and lawful brother of this Degree, or in a regularly constituted Lodge of Master Masons, nor unto him, or them, until by strict trial, due examination, or lawful information, I shall have found him, or them, as lawfully entitled to the same as I am myself.

"I furthermore promise and swear, that I will stand to and

abide by all laws, rules, and regulations of the Master Masons'
Degree, and of the Lodge of which I may hereafter become a member, as far as the same shall come to my knowledge; and that I will
ever maintain and support the constitution, laws, and edicts of the
Grand Lodge under which the same shall be holden.

"Further, that I will acknowledge and obey all due signs and
summonses sent to me from a Master Masons' Lodge, or given me
by a brother of that Degree, if within the length of my cable tow.

Candidate takes the oath of Master Mason

"Further, that I will always aid and assist all poor, distressed, worthy Master Masons, their widows and orphans, knowing them to be such, as far as their necessities may require, and my ability permit, without material injury to myself and family.

"Further, that I will keep a worthy brother Master Mason's secrets inviolable, when communicated to and received by me as such, murder and treason excepted.

"Further, that I will not aid, nor be present at, the initiation, passing, or raising of a woman, an old man in his dotage, a young man in his nonage, an atheist, a madman, or fool, knowing them to be such.

"Further, that I will not sit in a Lodge of clandestine-made Masons, nor converse on the subject of Masonry with a clandestine-made Mason, nor one who has been expelled or suspended from a Lodge, while under that sentence, knowing him or them to be such.

"Further, I will not cheat, wrong, nor defraud a Master Mason's Lodge, nor a brother of this Degree, knowingly, nor supplant him in any of his laudable undertakings, but will give him due and timely notice, that he may ward off all danger.

"Further, that I will not knowingly strike a brother Master Mason, or otherwise do him personal violence in anger, except in the necessary defence of my family or property.

"Further, that I will not have illegal carnal intercourse with a Master Mason's wife, his mother, sister, or daughter knowing them to be such, nor suffer the same to be done by others, if in my power to prevent.

"Further, that I will not give the Grand Masonic word, in any other manner or form than that in which I shall receive it, and then in a low breath.

"Further, that I will not give the Grand Hailing Sign of Distress except in case of the most imminent danger, in a just and lawful Lodge, or for the benefit of instruction; and if ever I should see it given, or hear the words accompanying it, by a worthy brother in distress, I will fly to his relief, if there is a greater probability of saving his life than losing my own.

"All this I most solemnly, sincerely promise and swear, with a firm and steady resolution to perform the same, without any hesitation, mental reservation, or secret evasion of mind whatever, binding myself, under no less penalty than that of having my body severed in two, my bowels taken from thence and burned to ashes, the ashes scattered before the four winds of heaven, that no more remembrance might be had of so vile and wicked a wretch as I would be, should I ever, knowingly, violate this my Master Mason's obligation. So help me God, and keep me steadfast in the due performance of the same."

The usual routine of asking for further light and removing the hoodwink follows the administration of the oath. He is shown how to wear the apron of a full fledged Mason and is told about the use of the trowel, the main third degree working tool. The Master tells the candidate he may retire to the anteroom while the lodge takes 30 minutes of refreshment, a Masonic term for recreation.

Unless forewarned the candidate may expect that nothing more remains but the usual platitudes in the charge. As a matter of fact the work on this final degree is just beginning. The altar, lights, and pillars are removed and some of the brethren fetch the paraphernalia used in the completion of the ceremony.

The candidate returns to the lodge room to receive the congratulations of the other members. They ask him how he enjoyed the work and if he is not glad it is through. The Master calls the lodge to "labor" and asks the Senior Warden, Junior Warden, and Secretary if they have any further business for the evening. They reply in the negative but the Master calls the candidate to his seat in the east. "Brother ——, I presume you now consider yourself a Master Mason, and, as such, entitled to all the privileges of a Master Mason, do you not?" He replies that he does.

"Brother ——, you are not yet a Master Mason, neither do I know that you ever will be, until I know how well you will withstand the amazing trials and dangers that await you. The Wardens and brethren of this Lodge require a more satisfactory proof of your fidelity to your trust, before they are willing to intrust you with the more valuable secrets of this Degree. You have a rough and rugged road to travel, beset with thieves, robbers, and murderers; and should you lose your life in the attempt, it will not be the first instance of the kind, my brother. You will remember in whom you put your trust, with that divine assurance, that 'he who endureth unto the end, the same shall be saved.' Heretofore you have had some one to pray for you, but now you have none. You must pray for yourself. You will therefore suffer yourself to be again hoodwinked, and kneel where you are, and pray orally or mentally, as you please. When through, signify by saying Amen, and arise and pursue your journey."

At this point the Junior Warden assumes the role of Jubela, the first ruffian, and grasps the blindfolded candidate by the collar. A dialogue follows.

Ruffian: Grand Master Miram Abiff, I am glad to meet you thus alone. I have long sought this opportunity. You will remember you promised us, that when the Temple was completed, we should receive the secrets of a Master Mason, whereby we might travel in foreign countries, work, and receive Master's wages. Behold! the Temple is now about to be completed, and we have not obtained that which we have so long sought. At first, I did not doubt your veracity; but now I do! I therefore now demand of you the secrets of a Master Mason!

Conductor (for candidate): Brother, this is an unusual way of asking for them. It is neither a proper time nor place; but be true to your engagement, and I will be true to mine. Wait until the Temple is completed, and then, if you are found worthy and well qualified, you will unquestionably receive the secrets of a Master Mason; but, until then, you cannot.

Ruffian: This does not satisfy me! Talk not to me of time or place, but give me the secrets of a Master Mason, or I will take your life!

Conductor: I cannot; nor can they be given, except in the presence of Solomon, king of Israel, Hiram, king of Tyre, and myself.

Ruffian: That does not satisfy me. I'll hear no more of your cavilling! Give me the Master's word, or I will take your life in a moment!

Conductor: I shall not!

Jubela brushes the candidate's throat with his hand and steps aside so that the conductor may shuffle the candidate along to the Senior Warden's station. The Senior Warden, playing the part of Jubelo, also seizes the candidate's collar and demands the secrets of a Master Mason. He brushes the left breast of the candidate who is hustled along to the Master's seat. The Master takes both collars of the candidate's coat while shouting, "You have escaped Jubela and Jubelo — me you cannot escape. My name is Jubelum. What I purpose, I perform. I hold in my hand an instrument of death; therefore, give me the secrets of a Master Mason, or I will take your life instantly!" The conductor answers for the jostled candidate, "I will not." Jubelum declares, "Then die!"

At this Jubelum hits the candidate a light blow on the head with a stuffed setting maul, pushes him backward and trips him so that he falls into a 7 ft. by 6 ft. canvas held by several of the brethren. He is lowered to the floor, bewildered and perhaps frightened. Remember that he is blindfolded.

Jubelum asks if he is dead and the brethren reply, "He is; his skull is broken in." Jubelum: "What horrid deed is this we have done? Brethren: We have murdered our Grand Master, Hiram Abiff, and have not obtained that which we have sought; this is not time for vain reflection — the question is, what shall we do with the body?" They decide to bury it in the rubbish of the Temple until low twelve when they plan to meet and give it a decent burial. The lodge becomes silent until the Master strikes the hour of low twelve (12 midnight) on a triangle or bell. The three ruffians appear to carry out the burial and a group of brethren hoist the canvas wrapped body of the candidate onto their shoulders and carry it around the lodge three times. They pretend to bury it and plant an acacia plant at the head in order to identify the spot. The conspirators plot to escape but are unable to deliver the pass needed to board a ship to Ethiopia; they decide to flee to the interior.

Now the remaining brethren begin to shout, laugh, and move about. They are supposed to be Temple workmen who report to the Master (who now plays King Solomon) that no work has been laid out on the trestle board and that they therefore have no work to do. A search is undertaken for Hiram and a roll call taken of the Fellow Crafts. They soon discover that the three assassins are absent. Meanwhile twelve Fellow Crafts are admitted to King Solomon's presence, kneel before him and confess that they and the three murderers entered into a conspiracy to extort the secrets of a Master Mason from Hiram but they chickened out. The King deputizes them to find the three escapees. Three of them sit down near the candidate, discover the newly planted acacia and hear the assassins accusing themselves of their crime. They overpower the ruffians and drag them to Solomon where they admit their guilt.

Jubelum taps candidate with a setting maul as members of the lodge wait to catch him in canvas

"Vile, impious wretches! despicable villains! reflect with horror on the atrocity of your crime, and on the amiable character of your Worshipful Grand Master, whom you have so basely assassinated. Hold up your heads, and hear your sentence. It is my orders that you be taken without the gates of the court, and be executed, according to your several imprecations, in the clefts of the rocks. Brother Junior Grand Warden, you will see my orders duly executed. Begone!"

The brethren rush into the anteroom and set up a clamor amid the groans of the "dying" ruffians. They return to tell Solomon that they have carried out the execution and he furthers orders them, "You twelve Fellow Crafts will go in search of the body, and, if found, observe whether the Master's word, or a key to it, or anything that appertains to the Master's Degree, is on or about it."

They stroll over to where the candidate lies shrouded in the canvas and discover the grave. "Here is the body of our Grand Master, Hiram Abiff, in a mangled and putrid state. Let us go and report. But what were our orders? We were ordered to observe whether the Master's word, or a key to it, or anything appertaining to the Master's Degree was on or about the body; but brother, we are only Fellow Crafts, and know nothing about the Master's word, or a key to it, or anything appertaining to the Master's Degree; we must, however, make an examination, or we will be put to death."

They fumble around the candidate's body and find the jewel which was attached to the yoke around his neck. "This is the jewel of his office" they exclaim and they detach the jewel and take it to King Solomon. They inform Solomon that they have been unable to find the Master's word and he tells the Treasurer: "My worthy brother of Tyre, as the Master's word is now lost, the first sign given at the grave and the first word spoken, after the body is raised, shall be adopted for the regulation of all Master's lodges, until future generations shall find out the right." By this the lodge hints at the discovery of the true Master's word which is given in the Royal Arch degree for those who wish to advance through the York rite.

All now form a circle around the body and sing the Masonic funeral dirge which is also used in Masonic burial services.

At the conclusion of the hymn the Master makes the grand hailing sign of distress by throwing both arms in the air. He exclaims, "O Lord my God, I fear the Master's word is lost forever." He tells the Junior Warden, "You will take the body by the Entered Apprentice grip, and see if it can be raised." He halfheartedly grasps the candidate's hand but lets it slip out. "Most Worshipful King Solomon, owing to the high state of putrefaction, it having been dead already fifteen days, the skin slips, and the body cannot be raised," he relates. The Master repeats the grand hailing sign and ejaculation and asks the Senior Warden to try raising the body with the Fellow Craft's grip. He too reports, "Owing to the reason given before, the flesh cleaves from the bone, and the body cannot be so raised." The Master wails, "O Lord my God; O Lord my God! O Lord my God! Is there no hope for the widow's son?" All kneel and repeat the following prayer:

"Thou, O God! knowest our down-sitting and our uprising, and understandest our thoughts afar off. Shield and defend us from the evil intentions of our enemies, and support us under the trials and afflictions we are destined to endure, while traveling through this vale of tears. Man that is born of a woman is of few days and full of trouble. He cometh forth as a flower, and is cut down: he fleeth also as a shadow, and continueth not. Seeing his days are determined, the number of his months are with thee; thou hast appointed his bounds that he cannot pass, turn from him that he may rest, till he shall accomplish his day. For there is hope of a tender branch thereof will not cease. But man dieth and wasteth away; yea, man giveth up the ghost, and where is he? As the waters fail from the sea, and the flood decayeth and drieth up, so man lieth down, and riseth not up till the heavens shall be no more. Yet, O Lord! have compassion on the children of thy creation, administer and comfort in time of trouble, and save them with an everlasting salvation. Amen."

Finally the Master sighs, "My worthy brother of Tyre, I shall endeavor to raise the body by the strong grip, or lion's paw, of the

Five points of fellowship

tribe of Judah." He grips the candidate with the Master Mason's grip and pulls him to his feet, giving him the grand Masonic word on the five points of fellowship. The word is "Ma-hah-bone" which the Master whispers to the candidate and asks him to repeat with him. The two exchange this word on the so-called five points of fellowship: foot to foot, knee to knee, breast to breast, hand to back and cheek to cheek or mouth to ear. The candidate's blindfold has been slipped off and he sees light for the first time in about an hour. The following explanation of the five points is given by the Master:

First: Foot to foot — that you will never hesitate to go on foot, and out of your way, to assist and serve a worthy brother.

Second: Knee to knee — that you will ever remember a brother's welfare, as well as your own, in all your adorations to Deity.

Third: Breast to breast — that you will ever keep in your breast a brother's secrets, when communicated to and received by you as such, murder and treason excepted.

Fourth: Hand to back — that you will ever be ready to stretch forth your hand to assist and save a fallen brother; and that you will vindicate his character behind his back, as well as before his face.

Fifth: Cheek to cheek, or mouth to ear — that you will ever caution and whisper good counsel in the ear of an erring brother, and, in the most friendly manner, remind him of his errors, and aid his reformation, giving him due and timely notice, that he may ward off approaching danger.

All the brethren take their seats while the candidate stands before the Master in the east and hears a lecture on the degree. This recounts the parts of the degree and the Hiram Abiff legend. He concludes by explaining the three grand Masonic pillars:

"The pillar of Wisdom represents Solomon, King of Israel, whose wisdom contrived the mighty fabric; the pillar of Strength, Hiram, King of Tyre, who strengthened Solomon in his grand undertaking; the pillar of Beauty, Hiram Abiff, the widow's son, whose cunning craft and curious workmanship beautified and adorned the Temple.

"The construction of this grand edifice was attended with two remarkable circumstances. From Josephus we learn, that although seven years were occupied in building it, yet, during the whole time, it rained not in the daytime, that the workmen might not be obstructed in their labor, and from sacred history it appears that there was neither the sound of hammer, nor axe, nor any tool of iron, heard in the house while it was building. This famous fabric was supported by fourteen hundred and fifty-three columns, and two thousand nine hundred and six pilasters — all hewn from the finest Parian marble.

"There were employed in its building three Grand Masters; three thousand three hundred Masters, or overseers of the work; eighty thousand Fellow Crafts, or hewers on the mountains and in the quarries; and seventy thousand Entered Apprentices, or bearers of burdens. All these were classes and arranged in such a manner, by the wisdom of Solomon, that neither envy, discord, nor confusion was suffered to interrupt that universal peace and tranquillity which pervaded the world at that important period.

"Brother ——, seven constitute a Lodge of Entered Apprentices — one Master Mason, and six Entered Apprentices. They usually meet on the Ground Floor of King Solomon's Temple.

"Five constitute a Lodge of Fellow Crafts — two Master Masons and three Fellow Crafts. They usually meet in the Middle Chamber of King Solomon's Temple.

"Three constitute a Lodge of Master Masons — three Master Masons. They meet in the Sanctum Sanctorum, or Holy of Holies of King Solomon's Temple."

He also explains more Masonic symbols such as the three steps, the pot of incense, beehive, book of constitutions, sword pointing to a naked heart, the all-seeing eye, the anchor and ark and the 47th problem of Euclid, the hourglass, scythe, setting maul, coffin, grave, acacia, and spade.

The Master delivers a charge to the lodge which follows:

"And now, my brethren, let us see to it, and so regulate our lives by the plumb-line of justice, ever squaring our actions by the square of virtue, that when the Grand Warden of Heaven may call for us, we may be found ready; let us cultivate assiduously the noble tenets of our profession — brotherly love, relief, and truth — and, from the square, learn morality; from the level, equality; from the plumb, rectitude of life. Let us imitate, in all his various perfections, him who, when assailed by the murderous band of rebellious craftsmen, maintained his integrity, even in death, and sealed his pledge with his own blood. Let us emulate his amiable and virtuous conduct, his unfeigned piety to his God, his inflexible integrity to his trust; and as the evergreen that bloomed at the head of the grave betokened the place of his interment, so may virtue's ever-blooming loveliness designate us as free and accepted Masons. With the trowel, spread liberally the cement of brotherly love and affection; and, circumscribed by the compass, let us ponder well our words and actions, and let all the energies of our minds and the affections of our souls be employed in the attainment of our Supreme Grand Warden's approbation. Thus, when dissolution draws nigh, and the cold winds of death come sighing around us, and his chilly dews already glisten on our foreheads, with joy shall we obey the summons of the Grand Warden of Heaven, and go from our labors on earth to everlasting refreshments in the Paradise of God. Then, by the benefit of the pass — a pure and blameless life — with a firm reliance on Divine Providence, shall we gain ready admission into that Celestial Lodge above, where the Supreme Grand Warden forever presides — forever reigns. When, placed at his right hand, he will be pleased to pronounce us just and upright Masons, then shall we be fitted as living stones for that spiritual temple, 'that house not made with hands, eternal in the heavens,' where no discordant voice shall be heard, but all the soul shall experience shall be perfect bliss, and all it shall express shall be perfect praise, and love divine shall ennoble every heart, and hallelujahs exalted employ every tongue."

The degree work concludes with the following charge to the newly made Master Mason:

"Brother, your zeal for the institution of Masonry, the progress you have made in the mystery, and your conformity to our regulations, have pointed you out as a proper object for our favor and esteem.

"You are now bound by duty, honor, and gratitude, to be faithful to your trust; to support the dignity of your character on every occasion; and to enforce, by precept and example, obedience to the tenets of the Order.

"In the character of a Master Mason, you are authorized to correct the errors and irregularities of your uninformed brethren, and to guard them against a breach of fidelity.

"To preserve the reputation of the fraternity unsullied must be your constant care; and, for this purpose, it is your province to recommend to your inferiors obedience and submission; to your equals, courtesy and affability; to your superiors, kindness and condescension. Universal benevolence you are always to cultivate; and, by the regularity of your own behavior, afford the best example for the conduct of others less informed. The ancient landmarks of the order, intrusted to your care, you are carefully to preserve; and never suffer them to be infringed, or countenance a deviation from the established usages and customs of the fraternity.

"Your virtue, honor, and reputation are concerned in supporting with dignity the character you now bear. Let no motive, therefore, make you swerve from your duty, violate your vows, or betray your trust; but be true and faithful, and imitate the example of that celebrated artist whom you this evening represent. Thus you will render yourself deserving of the honor which we have conferred, and merit the confidence we have reposed."

As usual there is a catechism or lecture which the candidate must commit to memory and recite at a later meeting. The candidate is now in possession of all Masonic secrets whose disclosure he has sworn to protect by a solemn oath given on the Holy Bible.

The monotony of these three degrees drives many older members to discontinue attending the lodge on any regular basis or to enter the Scottish and York rites in search of a greater variety and newer experience in Masonry.

CHAPTER IV

SCOTTISH AND YORK RITES

Master Masons Attend Graduate School

Most Masons go no further than the Blue Lodge (three degrees), but about one out of four elects to advance through either or both of the two principal systems of "higher degrees." Neither the Scottish rite nor the York rite constitutes an integral part of the Masonic order and neither is officially recognized by the Grand Lodges.

Claims of these two rites to form a part of Freemasonry rest only on the requirement that their initiates must be Master Masons. Expulsion from the so called "higher degrees" does not affect Blue Lodge membership. On the other hand, a Mason expelled from the Craft degrees is automatically excluded from the dependent "higher degrees." Therefore, membership in these higher degrees demands maintenance of membership in a Blue Lodge. Relations between the Blue Lodges and these rites are friendly, but a high ranking Scottish rite Mason or a Knight Templar exercises no precedence in local Blue Lodges nor may he wear his jewels of office or insignia of the rites in the Lodge.

In theory and in fact the individual state Grand Lodges are far more powerful than the Scottish rite. A Grand Master "outranks" any 33rd degree Mason. Of course, most state officers are also involved in the Scottish or York rites. Still, the Blue Lodge of three degrees is the basic unit of Masonry just as the parish is the basic unit of parochial organization and the Grand Lodge of each state is the Masonic "diocese."

Bernard E. Jones, author of the most reliable history of English Masonry, writes:

> The additional degrees are often called the "higher degrees," but the term seems hardly fair to "pure, ancient masonry." The "highest" degrees must always remain those which authentic masonic history proves to be the oldest. They are the three Craft degrees. Other degrees may be designated by higher numbers but in no sense other than, in some cases, that of a more highly developed symbolism, can they be said to be higher — a statement which does not in any way detract from their value or beauty. The Grand Lodges of England and of all English-speaking countries acknowledge the Craft degrees and, to a varying extent Royal Arch masonry and Mark masonry. All other degrees are "additional" or "side" degrees, and among them the Rose Croix and the Knights Templar occupy honoured and exceptional places.[1]

Nevertheless hundreds of thousands of Masons who are interested in acquiring the added prestige of the "higher degrees" and who are financially able to do so continue in one or both of the two rites. A Master Mason who wishes to become a 32nd degree Mason must pay an initiation fee of about $150 and spend four days of his time going through the ceremonies at a Scottish Rite cathedral. Those who choose to climb the ladder of the York or, as it is sometimes known, the American rite take a series of $10 and $15 degrees before becoming Knights Templar.

Some Masonic purists complain that many of their brethren enter the rites only to qualify for membership in the Shrine. Master Masons are repeatedly urged to take the "higher degrees." Louis B. Blakemore, president of the Masonic History Co., explains why many Blue Lodge Masons are induced to enter the rites:

> After taking his Third Degree the neophyte emerges considerably dazed in more ways than one. He then begins to wonder exactly what it means and what it is all about. At this point he is usually told that if he will just take the further or so called "higher" degrees all will be made clear to him, but neither the miscalled Scottish or York Rites ever throws, or even attempts to throw, much light upon the meaning of Symbolic Masonry.

---

[1] Bernard E. Jones, *Freemasons' Guide and Compendium* (London: George G. Harrap, 1950), p. 549.

Once Masonry was transplanted across the English Channel the French devotees set about devising literally hundreds of higher degrees. The manufacture and sale of spurious Masonic degrees proved profitable and the proprietors of various rites sought to control French Masonry by inventing higher and higher degrees. The surviving Scottish and York rites are only the two most successful of the dozens of rites which have sprung up. The 96-degree Rite of Memphis composed in France in 1838 is now extinct but a few exotic rites still claim followings especially in the Grand Orients.

The 33-degree system of the Ancient and Accepted Scottish Rite is built on the Rite of Perfection of 25 degrees devised in the college of Clermont in 1754. Some of the original degrees are said to have been composed by the Chevalier Ramsey, a Scotch Presbyterian turned Catholic, who attempted to use the new Masonic order to restore the Stuarts to the English throne.

In 1758 a body styling itself the *Conseils des Empereurs d'Orient et d'Occident* whose members were known as Sovereign Masonic Princes began to issue charters to work this Rite of Perfection. Three years later Stephen Morin, reportedly a Jew, was commissioned to propagate this rite in the Americas. He set up shop in Santo Domingo, West Indies, and conferred the degrees on Moses M. Hayes who appointed Isaac Da Costa as Deputy Inspector General for South Carolina. Within five years Morin was charged with "propagating strange and monstrous doctrines" and his charter was withdrawn. He disappeared from the scene.

The Grand Lodge of Perfection was established at Charleston, S. C., in 1783 and became the Supreme Council in 1801. John Mitchell and the Rev. Frederick Dalcho, an Episcopalian clergyman, headed this new Council. Four Jews and three Christians completed the Council's roster. Although the English branch of the Ancient and Accepted Rite is closed to non-Christians, the parent Supreme Council has never set up a Christian qualification for admittance.

Eight degrees imported from Europe were added to the reshuffled 25 degrees of the Rite of Perfection in 1802. In order to justify this action the legend was planted that a 33-degree system had been authorized by Frederick the Great of Prussia who became the posthumous patron of the rite. Frederick had dabbled in Masonry at one time but soon lost interest in the lodge and had died in 1786. The patriarch of the Scottish Rite, Albert Pike, admits, "There is no doubt that Frederick came to the conclusion that the great pretensions of Masonry in the blue degrees were merely imaginary and deceptive. He ridiculed the Order and thought its ceremonies mere child's play; and some of his sayings to that effect have been preserved." No Masonic historian now regards the part played by Frederick in the formation of the Scottish rite as anything but mythical. The kindest word which may be said for those who perpetrated this hoax is that they considered such a fraud essential to entice Masons to purchase their degrees.

A Northern Jurisdiction dividing roughly along the Mason Dixon line and the Mississippi River began to function in 1813 and now maintains headquarters in Boston, while the Southern Jurisdiction has moved from Charleston to Washington, D. C. The latter embraces 33 Southern and Western states including Minnesota, Iowa, and North Dakota. The Northern branch now claims 460,000 members in 14 other states and the Southern Jurisdiction about 450,000.

Pike must be credited with bringing the Scottish rite to the position of prestige it occupies today. It is said that he found Masonry in a log cabin and left it in a temple. A teacher-trapper-journalist-lawyer-poet-Confederate general, Pike busied himself in the fields of esoteric Masonry and Oriental religion. Regarding esoteric Masonry he had the field pretty much to himself since few men of learning would bother with the fables and pretensions of the Craft. Religiously Pike was more of an occultist and pagan than a Christian and his personal philosophy was woven into his revisions of the Scottish rite rituals, especially those of the Southern Jurisdiction which he served as Grand Commander for 32 years from 1859. His *Morals and Dogma*, a turgid 861-page commentary on the 33 degrees, is still the standard monitor and copies are usually presented to new 14th degree members.

Pike seemed to challenge the adequacy of Blue Lodge Masonry when he wrote:

> The Blue Degrees are but the outer court or portico of the Temple. Part of the symbols are displayed there to the Initiate, but he is intentionally misled by false interpretations. It is not intended that he shall understand them; but it is intended that he shall imagine he understands them. Their true explication is reserved for the Adepts, the Princes of Masonry . . . it is well enough for the mass of those called Masons, to imagine that all is contained in the Blue Degrees; and whoso attempts to undeceive them will labor in vain and without true reward violate his obligation as an Adept.[2]

We must realize, of course, that Pike was selling his particular brand of "higher" Masonry although his patronizing attitude toward other Masons and his frank admissions of deceit and false interpretations must annoy many brethren. He had to dangle a carrot before Masons who were quite satisfied to remain in Craft Masonry.

While the York rite, culminating in the Knights Templar degree, refuses admission to any but Christian Masons, the Scottish rite in the United States repudiates any specifically Christian qualification. "All the Degrees of Scottish Masonry can be received by good men of every race and religious faith; and any Degree that cannot be so received is not Masonry, which is universal, but some other thing that is exclusive and therefore intolerant. All our degrees have, in that, one object. Each inculcates toleration, and the union of men of all faiths; and each erects a platform on which the Mohammedan, the Israelite, and the Christian may stand side by side and hand in hand, as true brethren."[3]

Various elaborations on the King Solomon's Temple theme and certain occult material are illustrated in the Scottish rite degrees. Mackey states, "Some of these legends have concurrent support of Scripture; some are related by Josephus; and some appear to have no historical foundation." Several of the degrees describe the vengeance wreaked on the assassins of Hiram Abiff: Jubela, Jubelo, and Jubelum.

---

[2] Albert Pike, *Morals and Dogma*, p. 819.
[3] *Liturgy of the Ancient and Accepted Scottish Rite of Freemasonry for the Southern Jurisdiction of the U.S.A.* (1936), Part III, p. 173.

Since the working of the Scottish rite degrees demands elaborate props, costumes, scenery, furniture, and trap doors, the Scottish rite cathedrals are found only in the larger cities and draw on a membership in a large radius. Several hundred men may advance from Master Mason to 32nd degree in ceremonies which typically consume four days and nights to complete. Most of the initiates watch the proceedings from the sidelines while small groups of a dozen men may go through a particular degree as representatives of the entire class.

In England the Ancient and Accepted Rite was introduced from America in 1846 but dropped the title "Scottish" in 1909. Only Christians may take the 18th or Rose Croix degree and therefore all 32nd and 33rd degree Masons in that country are Christians. The English rite works only the 18th, 30th, 31st, and 32nd degrees, the others being conferred titularly. The English rite limits the number of 31st degree Masons to 600, 32nd to 250, and 33rd to 70 plus eight honorary 33rds.

Both the Scottish and York rites have waived the right to confer the basic three degrees. The Blue Lodges would certainly not appreciate any encroachment on these grounds. In the Northern Jurisdiction of the Scottish rite the 4th to 14th degrees (see page 7) are conferred in a Lodge of Perfection. The next two degrees are conferred in a Council, Princes of Jerusalem. A Chapter of Rose Croix de H-R-D-M controls the Apocalyptic and so-called Christian Grades, the 17th and 18th degrees. Finally, a Consistory, Sublime Princes of the Royal Secret, controls the 19th through 32nd degrees. The 33rd degree is purely honorary and is bestowed on a limited number of 32nd degree Masons each year who have distinguished themselves as Masons. In 1949 there were 4300 33rds in the United States, most of whom were known as honorary rather than active 33rds. They included, among others, President Harry S. Truman, Gen. Douglas MacArthur, FBI Director J. Edgar Hoover, Chief Justice Earl Warren.

At the biennial session of the Southern Supreme Council in 1957, 359 men were elected to receive the 33rd degree and another 1261 32nd degree members were awarded a consolation prize in the form of the decoration of Knight Commander of the Court of Honour. Among the new 33rd degree members were a senator and a congressman from Arkansas, the Commanding General of Walter Reed Army Medical Center, the superintendents of schools of Washington, D. C., and St. Louis, a congressman from Kansas and another from Oklahoma, a railroad president, and a psychiatrist. The Northern Jurisdiction chose 188 candidates to be coronated as 33rd degree Masons during 1958.

Dozens of oaths are administered in progressing through the series of Scottish rite degrees. A sample oath would be that of the 10th degree, Master Elect of Fifteen:

> I, ——, do promise and swear upon the Holy Bible, never to reveal where I have received this degree, nor even say who assisted at my reception, and I furthermore promise never to receive any in this degree without a full power from my superiors. Nor to assist at any reception unless in a regular manner and Chapter of this degree. To keep exactly in my heart all the secrets that shall be revealed to me. And in failure of this, my obligation, I consent to have my body opened perpendicularly, and to be exposed for eight hours in the open air, that the venemous flies may eat of my entrails, my head to be cut off and put on the highest pinnacle of the world, and I will always be ready to inflict the same punishment on those who shall disclose this degree and break this obligation. So may God help and maintain me. Amen.

Hiram's assassins get their comeuppance in the 11th degree when they are ripped open from the chin downward to allow flies to suck their blood. The Royal Arch degree of the York rite is altered and becomes the 13th degree of the Ancient and Accepted Rite. In the final or 14th degree of the Chapter the candidates agree to assemble at the lodge on December 27, feast of St. John the Evangelist, and on June 24, feast of St. John the Baptist.

Masons sometimes point to the 18th degree of the Rose Croix as an example of the "Christian" orientation of the "higher" degrees. We know, however, that Jews, Unitarians, and Moslems are not debarred from any degree in the Scottish rite and we presume they would not participate in a ceremony which offended their religious beliefs. Incidentally, the candidate is asked, "Do you promise never to consent to the admission into a Chapter of

Rose Croix of anyone who is or has been a Monk or Jesuit, or is an Atheist?"

The Rose Croix candidate passes through three apartments, representing Calvary, the scene of the Ascension, and hell. The initiate is warned, "The horrors (of hell) which you have just seen are but a faint representation of those you shall suffer if you break through our laws, or infringe the obligation you have taken."

A Mason who belonged to a Christian denomination might well be deceived by the symbols used in this ceremony. He sees a cross and may understandably associate this with the Christian religion until he reads in his copy of Morals and Dogma:

> The Cross has been a sacred symbol from the earliest Antiquity. It is found upon all the enduring monuments of the world, in Egypt, in Assyria, in Hindostan, in Persia, and on the Buddhist towers of Ireland [!]. Buddha was said to have died upon it. The Druids cut an oak into its shape and held it sacred, and built their temples in that form. Pointing to the four quarters of the world, it was the symbol of universal nature. It was on a cruciform tree, that Chrishna was said to have expired, pierced with arrows. It was revered in Mexico. But its peculiar meaning in this degree, is that given by the Ancient Egyptians.[4]

Well, perhaps the Rose Croix is not the Christian symbol we might have imagined but what about the Sacred Word of the degree: I.N.R.I.? Again the leading authority on Scottish rite Masonry enlightens us:

> To the word INRI, inscribed on the Crux Ansata over the Master's Seat, many meanings have been assigned. The Christian Initiate reverentially sees in it the initials of the inscription upon the cross on which Christ suffered — Iesus Nazarenus Rex Iudaeorum. The sages of Antiquity connected it with one of the greatest secrets of Nature, that of universal regeneration. They interpreted it thus, Igne Natura renovatur integra (entire nature is renovated by fire): The Alchemical or Hermetic Masons framed for it this aphorism, Igne nitrum roris invenitur. And the Jesuits are charged with having applied to it this odious axiom, Justum necare reges impios. The four letters are the initials of the Hebrew words that represent the four elements — Iammim, the seas or water; Nour, fire; Rouach, the air, and Iebeschah, the dry earth. How we read it, I need not repeat to you.[5]

---

[4] Albert Pike, Morals and Dogma, p. 290.
[5] Ibid., p. 291.

Needless to say, Pike and his cronies of the Scottish rite do not read it as "Christian Initiates."

On Maundy Thursday members of the Rose Croix chapters celebrate the Feast of the Paschal Lamb with a 1½-hour ceremony combining Jewish and Christian elements. Thirteen members wearing dark robes represent participants at the Last Supper and sit at a cross-shaped table.

Undoubtedly the most objectionable degree in the Scottish rite is the 30th or Grand Elect Knight Kadosh K-H or simple Knight Kadosh in the Southern Jurisdiction. Candidates may skip the previous 11 degrees in order to take the 30th which is never conferred titularly. Vengeance is the motif of this degree, whose bitterly anti-Catholic tone is absent in the corresponding English workings.

The Thrice Puissant Grand Master charges the candidates: "Your assistance at this juncture is invaluable, as we have crime to punish and innocence to protect. Persecution and oppression are raging. The religious and political rulers of the world will not render that justice which they have sworn to render, and we cannot endure their encroachments any longer." The Grand Master approaches a table which supports three skulls. One skull wears a papal tiara, another a wreath of laurel, and the third a regal crown. The Grand Master stabs the skull with the papal tiara and the candidate repeats, "Down with Imposture! Down with crime!" Both the Grand Master and candidate kneel before the second skull and chorus "Everlasting glory to the immortal martyr of virtue." Passing to the third crowned skull the two repeat, "Down with tyranny! Down with crime!"

The Grand Pontiff addresses the candidate:

"You have already been informed that among the Knights Kadosh truth and reality take the place of symbols, and even now your sagacity will partly raise the curtain which cannot be entirely removed until you have sustained new trials. In all the preceding degrees you must have observed that the object of Scotch Masonry is to overthrow all kinds of superstition, and that by admitting in her bosom on terms of the strictest equality, the members of all religions, of all creeds and of all countries, without any distinction whatever, she has, and indeed can have, but one single object and that is to restore to the Grand Architect of the Universe, to the common father of the human race those who are lost in the maze of impostures, invented for the sole purpose of enslaving them. The Knights Kadosh recognize no particular religion, and for that reason we demand of you nothing more than to worship God. And whatever may be the religious forms imposed upon you by superstition at a period of your life when you were incapable of discerning truth from falsehood, we do not even require you to relinquish them. Time and study alone can enlighten you. But remember that you will never be a true Mason unless you repudiate forever all superstitions and prejudices.

"However, until then, you will own that we have required of you nothing more than to acknowledge with us the sole, the only certain and undoubted point admitted as such by all the human race without exception. We mean the existence of a first great cause, whom we call God Almighty."

The candidate now takes his second oath as a Knight Kadosh:

"I, ——, solemnly and sincerely promise and swear wholly to devote myself to the emancipation of humanity; to practice toleration, in political and religious matters especially, toward all men. To strive unceasingly for the happiness of my fellow beings, for the propagation of light and for the overthrow of superstition, fanaticism, imposture, and intolerance.

"I furthermore solemnly promise and swear to help my brethren even at the peril of my life, if they should be persecuted for their religion, for the holy cause of liberty, or as members of the higher Masonic bodies. So help me God."

The Grand Pontiff now instructs the candidate to toss some incense in the fire burning on the altar of perfumes while he prays, "Almighty Father, Holy and Merciful. Oh! Thou of whom we are the beloved children, accept this incense which we offer thee with our hearts, as a token of love and reverence. May thy kingdom come at last, and with it the end of all fanaticism, intolerance, imposture, and superstition. Amen."

In a subsequent mock balloting on the candidate's fitness one of the Judges reports, "I have voted in the negative, Sovereign Grand Judge. I have good reason to believe, nay I know, that the candidate entertains anti-Masonic opinions; that is to say, intolerant and sectarian principles, not only in religious but also in Masonic matters." The dissenting Judge asks that the candidate compose a written testament of his profession of faith in Masonry. The candidate complies with this demand and the document is kept on file in the Scottish Rite Cathedral.

As the Grand Provost of Justice points a sword at the heart of the candidate he repeats his third oath as Knight Kadosh:

"I, ——, of my own free will and accord, do hereby solemnly and sincerely promise and swear to keep faithfully the secrets of the sublime degree of Knight Kadosh and strictly to obey the statutes of the order.

"I further solemnly promise and swear to protect innocence and to punish crime, to help all in distress, to do all in my power to crush oppressors and to defend the oppressed. Every Knight Kadosh shall be to me as if the ties of blood had united us.

"I further solemnly promise and swear never to challenge a Knight Kadosh to mortal combat, before having previously submitted my motives to the Council assembled in its Areopagus, and if I were in a place where no Council existed, to take advice of at least two Knights Kadosh.

"I furthermore solemnly promise and swear never to slander a Knight Kadosh, and never to cause him any prejudice either by word or by action. And should I ever infringe or violate any of my obligations I now take, I do from this moment accept and consent to undergo the sentence which may be pronounced against me by this dreaded tribunal, which I hereby acknowledge as my Supreme Judge. All of which I promise to do, under the penalty of death. So help me God."

A large mausoleum in the shape of a pyramid is featured in the fourth apartment which is hung with red and black draperies. A funeral urn crowned with laurel and covered by a black veil rests on a platform of the mausoleum flanked by the papal tiara and the royal crown. Thick incense obscures the interior of the hall which is illuminated by only five candles. An altar on the west holds a human skull inlaid with silver, a decanter of wine and a loaf of bread covered by a cloth. A ladder with seven rungs is placed between the mausoleum and the altar.

The candidate for Knight Kadosh is instructed to ascend the ladder. Each step on one side represents a quality such as Justice and Meekness while the reverse steps stand for a science such as Geometry. Following the fourth oath the candidate is told, "My brother, you are now convinced that the degree of Knight Kadosh is the apex of the Masonic edifice. It contains all the science of Masonry." Of course, this claim is rejected by the Blue Lodges which do not even officially acknowledge the existence of degrees other than the basic three.

The Thrice Puissant Grand Master points to the papal tiara and declares:

"This represents the tiara of the cruel and cowardly Pontiff, who sacrificed to his ambition the illustrious order of those Knights Templar of whom we are the true successors. A crown of gold and precious stones ill befits the humble head of one who pretends to be the successor, the Vicar, of Jesus of Nazareth. It is therefore the crown of an impostor, and it is in the name of Him who said, 'Neither be ye called Masters' that we trample it under our feet."

He asks if the candidate is willing to do this and then all trample on the pope's crown, brandishing poniards and shouting "Down with Imposture!" Did we understand Pike correctly when he said that men of all races and creeds may take the Scottish rite degrees without compromising their beliefs? We know that Negroes are barred from the Scottish rite and we feel justified in doubting the faith of any Catholic who would insult the emblem of the pope's authority in a lodge ritual.

Earlier in the 30th degree ritual the prospective Knights Kadosh are counseled, "And, finally, keep aloof from uniting yourself with any sectional, political, or sectarian religious organization whose principles can in any way bias your mind or judgment, or in the slightest degree trammel with obligations the vows you have just made." This leaves no question of which society, Church or Scottish rite, should claim a man's first loyalty. President Charles A. Blanchard of Wheaton College pointed out, "Not less than five or six times in the dreary monotony of this degree is the candidate given to understand that Christianity is a narrow, fanatical, intolerant system while Masonry is a broad, comprehensive, generous one, and that if he is a good Mason he must not be a Christian."

This blasphemy is delivered by the Advocate in the working of the 31st degree, "We revolt against the law, by which the crooked limbs and diseased organism of the child are the fruits of the father's vices. We even think that a God, omnipotent and omniscient, ought to have permitted no pain, no poverty, no servitude. Our ideal of justice is more lofty than the actualities of God."

A recital of the lessons of the preceding 31 degrees begins the initiation ceremony of the 32nd degree, the goal of most Scottish rite aspirants. The candidates are told that "Masonry will eventually rule the world" and they pray for the "universal dominion of the true principles of Masonry."

A select few, known for their devotion to Masonic principles, are chosen each year to receive the honorary 33rd degree. In this ceremony the Grand Master of Ceremonies unveils a skeleton with a wreath of cypress in one hand and the banner of the order in the other. The candidate embraces the skeleton and drinks from a human skull. The Most Puissant Sovereign Grand Commander explains, "Sublime Prince, the Ancient and Accepted Rite recognizes and adopts none of the religions of the world. We respect the creeds of all men, because God alone is the Supreme Judge of His children. Each of our brethren has full right to maintain his own faith and worship of our Heavenly Father according to the dictates of his own conscience." He then asks, "What is your religion?" The candidate responds and the appropriate book of scriptures is produced and placed on the altar. The candidate then takes his last oath in the Scottish system on the Bible, Pentateuch, Koran, Vedas, or whatever book he considers holy.

The chart on page 7 indicates the names of all the degrees in Scottish rite Masonry. A slightly different arrangement prevails in the Southern Jurisdiction. Degrees 15 through 18 are conferred in a Chapter of Rose Croix, 19 through 30 by a Council of Kadosh, and 31 and 32 by a Consistory. In some cases the name of the degree also varies.

The *Encyclopedia Americana* explains, "Though founded on Craft Masonry, the Scottish rite is not so much a branch thereof as it is a separate system of Masonry; entirely so as to organization, and largely so as to doctrine."[6] The Scottish rite is not bound by the Masonic landmark which outlaws discussion of politics and religion in the lodge. As a result what anti-Catholic propaganda is disseminated in American Freemasonry may usually be traced to the Scottish rite, particularly the Southern Jurisdiction. The Mason who has never gone beyond the Blue Lodge may be quite sincere when he testifies that he has never heard a word against the Church in his lodge. But the Southern Jurisdiction Scottish rite Mason who would make the same statement would be unusually inattentive or else simply evasive.

The Southern Jurisdiction publishes the monthly *New Age* which boasts a record of anti-Catholicism unsurpassed by any other publication and seldom equaled even by the Ku Klux Klan periodicals of the 1920's or by the notorious *Menace*.

The Scottish rite has taken a particular interest in the George Washington University in Washington, D. C., and has so far given $1,400,000 to the school's endowment. The Scottish Rite Foundation granted $10,000 to Baylor University in 1957 to sponsor a chair for Church-State studies. The Foundation responded to an appeal by Baylor President W. R. White 33° who pointed out, "Baylor has had both a Masonic and a Baptistic leadership since its origin 112 years ago." A similar grant, in this case $20,000, went to the American University to underwrite a professorship in American studies. The rite encourages Masons and Protestants to enter federal employment, especially the state department, to offset a supposed influx of Georgetown-trained Catholics. Scottish rite Masons operate hospitals for crippled children in Texas, Georgia, and Colorado and a dormitory for 345 coeds with Masonic connections at the University of Texas.

---

[6] *Encyclopedia Americana*, Vol. 18, p. 389a.

Other Master Masons may choose to advance through the 10-degree York rite of which three degrees may be skipped. As the Scottish rite has nothing to with Scotland so the York rite has nothing to do with York. A more accurate but less popular term is the American rite since this combination of degrees is worked only in the United States.

Three preparatory degrees of Mark Master, Past Master (Virtual), and Most Excellent Master culminate in the Royal Arch degree. In England this Royal Arch degree has been considered a complementary degree to the third degree since the 1813 reconciliation. As such it claims to be a part of pure and ancient Masonry. With 800,000 members the Royal Arch is the largest body within American Freemasonry. It and the three preceding York rite degrees are controlled by the General Grand Chapter of Royal Arch Masons of the United States of America.

The quest for the true name of God forms the basis for the Royal Arch degree which seems to have been introduced into modern Masonry in the 1750's. According to Masonic legend God's name, revealed to Moses in the burning bush, was known to the Jews until the assassination of Hiram Abiff. At Hiram's death a substitute name "Mahabone" was invented but the real name was not discovered until 470 years later in the building of the second temple. JAH-BUL-ON, the supposed lost word, is made up of three ancient names for the deity, the Hebrew Jehovah, the Assyrian Baal, and the Egyptian On or Osiris. This linking of the sacred name of the God of the Hebrews with the names of two pagan deities shocked even Pike who wrote, "No man or body of men can make me accept as a sacred word, as a symbol of the infinite and eternal Godhead, a mongrel word, whose name has been for more than two thousand years an appellation of the Devil." He added, "No word has any business in the Royal Arch degree that makes the name of a heathen deity one of the names of the true God."

The lengthy oath administered by the Principal Sojourner and repeated by the Royal Arch candidate includes the following statement: "I furthermore promise and swear that I will employ a

Companion Royal Arch Mason in preference to any other person of equal qualifications. I furthermore promise and swear that I will assist a Companion Royal Arch Mason when I see him engaged in any difficulty, and will espouse his cause so far as to extricate him from the same, whether he be right or wrong."

Should the York rite Mason wish, he may apply for the trio of wearisome Council degrees: Royal Master, Select Master, and Super Excellent Master but he can also bypass these and move directly into the Commandery. A class of York rite candidates may receive the Chapter degrees on a Wednesday evening and Thursday followed by the Council degrees on Friday night and the Commandery degrees on Saturday.

The top degree of the York rite is the Knights Templar but the prospective Templar must also enter the Order of the Red Cross and the Order of Knights of Malta. The scene between Christ and Thomas is re-enacted in the Knights of Malta ritual; the candidate puts his fingers into the print of nails in the Eminent Commander's hands. The York rite's Red Cross of Constantine corresponds to the honorary 33rd degree of the Scottish rite.

Not a shred of evidence supports the claim that the Masonic Knights Templar represents the modern successor to this suppressed medieval order. A gap of more than 500 years separates the two orders but as usual the demands of historical accuracy are not oppressive in Masonic research. The original order was formed to protect Christian pilgrims in the Holy Land. Noblemen entered its ranks and took vows of poverty, chastity, and obedience. Eventually the income of this quasi-religious order reached huge proportions and oriental heresies were said to have infected some of the high officials. Grand Knight Jacques DeMolay and 60 Knights were arrested in Paris and charged with idolatry. DeMolay and 54 of the Knights were burned at the stake in 1314; the order was suppressed by Church and State and its possessions were confiscated. The Masonic imitation was organized in the United States in 1816.

Early in the Templar initiation ceremony the candidate is seated blindfolded in the Chamber of Reflection. When he removes his hoodwink he sees a Bible, a bowl of water and napkin, and a skull and cross bones. He is asked to complete a questionnaire which asks, "Should you ever be called upon to draw your sword, will you wield it in the defence of the Christian religion?" At the conclusion of the Knight Templar's obligation the new Knight swears, "All this I most solemnly and sincerely promise and vow, with a firm and steadfast resolution to keep and perform the same, binding myself under no less penalty than that of having my head smote off and placed on the highest spire of Christendom, should I ever willfully or knowingly violate any part of this solemn obligation of a Knight Templar, so help me God and keep me steadfast to keep and perform the same."

The candidate drinks wine libations to the memory of "our ancient Grand Master, Solomon, King of Israel," to Hiram, King of Tyre, and to Hiram Abiff. After the third libation the Eminent Commander reminds the candidates: "Pilgrim, these libations in honor of the illustrious Grand Masters of Ancient Craft Masonry are taken in acknowledgement of our connection with, and veneration for, that ancient and honorable institution; but the order to which you now seek to unite is founded upon the Christian religion and the practice of the Christian virtues; you will therefore attend to a lesson from the holy evangelist." He reads Matthew 26:14–25.

The candidate faces a triangular arrangement of 12 candles to represent the 12 Apostles. In the center of the table a skull rests on a Bible. In memory of the apostasy of Judas the candidate is asked to extinguish one of the tapers "and let it teach you this important lesson, that he who would violate his vow or betray his trust is worthy of no better fate than that which Judas suffered."

The fourth libation to Simon of Cyrene is drunk from a skull and the fifth, of pure wine, is drunk to immortality. "This pure wine I now take in testimony of my belief in the mortality of the body and the immortality of the soul; and as the sins of the whole world were once visited upon the head of our Savior, so may all the sins of the person whose skull this once was, in addition to my own, be heaped upon my head, and may this libation appear in judgment against me, both here and hereafter, should I ever knowingly or willfully violate this my most solemn vow of a Knight

Templar; so help me God and keep me steadfast." To enforce the fifth libation the assembled Knights draw swords and point them toward the candidate's throat.

The medieval Knight Templar was received into the order: "In the name of God, and of Mary our dear Lady, and in the name of St. Peter of Rome, and of our father the Pope, and in the name of all the brethren of the Temple, we receive you to all the good works of the order." The Masonic Knights Templar employ the following formula: "By virtue of the high power and authority in me vested as the representative of Hugh de Payens and Geoffrey de St. Omer, I do now dub and create you, ——, a Knight of this most valiant and magnanimous order of Knights Templar."

Some 400,000 Knights Templar are banded together in 300 Commanderies in the United States, Alaska, Mexico, the Philippine Islands, and the Canal Zone. Knights wear a black military uniform with cocked hat and ostrich feathers, silver and gold belts, and swords. They attend Protestant church services in a body on Ascension Day. Their marching hymn is "Onward, Christian Soldiers."

Some Masons attain the 32nd and 33rd degrees in the Scottish rite and then begin to climb the York rite ladder or vice versa. By this time they have invested hundreds of dollars in initiation fees, dues, emblems, assessments, banquets, costumes, travel expenses, etc. Most of those who have reached the top degrees in either of the two rites also enter the Shrine.

Our thesis that Freemasonry and Christianity form mutually incompatible systems is neither advanced nor rebutted by the contents of the "higher degrees." Most Masons have no knowledge of these rites and the Blue Lodges of Craft Masonry simply ignore their existence. Neither the objectionable occultism and paganism of some Scottish rite degrees nor the Christian coloring of the Knights Templar have anything to do with our argument. To the general public, however, all these assorted rites, allied degrees, and the Shrine are "Masonry" and a basic knowledge of them becomes necessary if we wish to understand the complexities of American Freemasonry.

CHAPTER V

THE MASONIC RELIGION

Masonry Encompasses All Elements of a Religion of Naturalism

The basic Christian objection to Freemasonry is that the Craft constitutes a religious sect in opposition to the revealed truths of the Gospel. Whatever the religious doctrines of the Masonic sect it is plain that they do not embrace the central Christian doctrines of the Trinity, the Fall, the Incarnation, the Atonement. To the lodge these essential Christian beliefs are completely irrelevant. No one need accept the Christian revelation, acknowledge Jesus Christ as God and Man, or receive baptism in order to attain salvation and enjoy the eternal happiness promised by the lodge.

Not all the religious systems in the world are exclusive; Christianity is. A Chinese may combine elements of Confucianism, Buddhism, and Taoism and a Japanese may successfully blend Shintoism and Buddhism. A Christian owes complete loyalty to Jesus Christ, God made man; he may not divide his allegiance among other gods.

Most Masons who deny that Masonry is a religion confuse religion with the Christian religion. They know Masonry is not Christian since if it were their Jewish and Moslem brethren would object. Since it is not Christian they assume that it is not religious. Or their views of Christianity as primarily a system of character building and as synonymous with the decent, kindly, and gentlemanly coincide

71

with their appraisal of the lodge and they see no conflict between
the two institutions. The fact is, however, that the lodge is
essentially religious and possesses all the elements of a religion of
naturalism.

Masons themselves have testified again and again to the religious
nature of the lodge while denying that Masonry should be classified
as "sectarian" religion. By this they mean that the various religious
faiths represent on a lower plane that pure and undefiled universal
religion of mankind represented by Freemasonry. For example,
Pike states:

> Masonry is not a religion. He who makes of it a religious belief
> falsifies and denaturalizes it. The Brahmin, the Jew, the Mohometan,
> the Catholic, the Protestant, each professing his peculiar religion,
> sanctioned by the laws, by time, and by climate, must needs retain
> it, and cannot have two religions; for the social and sacred laws
> adapted to the usages, manners, and prejudices of particular countries
> are the work of man.[1]

Masonry is willing to humor those brethren who go along with
the local and tribal cults so long as they realize that the sectarian
doctrines of these cults are simply necessary evils. Pike explains:

> But Masonry teaches, and has preserved in their purity, the cardinal
> tenets of the old primitive faith, which underlie and are the founda-
> tion of all religion. All that ever existed have had a basis of truth;
> and all have overlaid that truth with errors . . . Masonry is the
> universal morality which is suitable to the inhabitants of every clime,
> to the man of every creed.[2]

He adds, "Religion, to obtain currency and influence with the
great mass of mankind, must needs be alloyed with such an amount
of error as to place it far below the standard attainable by the higher
human capacities."[3] Masonry, however, strips sectarian religion of
these encrusted errors and reveals itself as the universal religion.
While religion gathers the barnacles of superstition and error,
Masonry remains pure and undefiled. It becomes Christianity without Christ, Judaism without the Law, Islam without the Prophet.

---

[1] Albert Pike, *Morals and Dogma*, p. 161.
[2] *Ibid.*
[3] *Ibid.*, p. 224.

Some Masonic partisans seem to believe that Masonry could not qualify as a religion because it lacks the complex dogmatic systems of the denominations in their hometown. The lodge demands only belief in a Supreme Architect and in the immortality of the soul. As Mackey states: "The religion of Masonry is pure theism." He boasts, "The truth is that Masonry is undoubtedly a religious institution . . . which, handed down through a long succession of ages from that ancient priesthood who first taught it, embraces the great tenets of the existence of God and the immortality of the soul."[4] In his *Encyclopedia* he restates this: "The Religious Doctrines of Freemasonry are very simple and self evident. They are darkened by no perplexities of sectarian theology but stand out in broad light, intelligible and acceptable by all minds, for they ask only for a belief in God and in the immortality of the soul."[5]

> Although Freemasonry is not a dogmatic theology, and is tolerant in the admission of men of every religious faith, it would be wrong to suppose that it is without a creed. On the contrary, it has a creed, the assent to which it rigidly enforces, and the denial of which is absolutely incompatible with membership in the Order. This creed consists of two articles: First, a belief in God, the Creator of all things, who is therefore recognized as the Grand Architect of the Universe; and secondly, a belief in the eternal life, to which this present life is but a preparatory and probationary state.[6]

Simply because Masonry reduces its theological statement to these two propositions we may not deduce that it does not constitute a religion. This bare minimum compared to the dogmatic structure of Christianity is nevertheless more than is asked of many religionists: Unitarians, Reform Jews, Buddhists. A Unitarian in good standing may doubt the existence of a personal God and flatly deny the immortality of the soul; his Unitarianism nevertheless constitutes a religion.

Like Unitarianism the Masonic sect denies the need to accept the Christian gospel but allows its initiates to entertain their own peculiar theological views outside the lodge room. Human reason

---

[4] Albert G. Mackey, *Textbook of Masonic Jurisprudence*, p. 95.
[5] Albert G. Mackey, *Encyclopedia of Freemasonry*, p. 731.
[6] *Ibid.*, p. 192.

becomes the only guide to religious belief and the gospel of Christ stands on a par with the scriptures of Hinduism, the Koran, and the Book of Mormon.

The lodge unwittingly confirmed the religious nature of Masonry in a court case in 1903. A certain Robert Kopp, who had been expelled from the fraternity, appealed against his former brethren in the civil courts. He lost his case but the counsel for the Grand Lodge of New York presented the following statement in his "Briefs and Points":

> The right to membership in the Masonic fraternity is very much like the right to membership in a church. Each requires a candidate for admission to subscribe to certain articles of religious belief as an essential prerequisite to membership. Each requires a member to conduct himself thereafter in accordance with certain religious principles. Each requires its members to adhere to certain doctrines of belief and action. The precepts contained in the "Landmarks and the Charges of a Freemason" formulate a creed so thoroughly religious in character that it may well be compared with the formally expressed doctrine of many a denominational church. The Masonic fraternity may, therefore, be quite properly regarded as a religious society, and the long line of decisions, holding that a religious society shall have sole and exclusive jurisdiction to determine matters of membership, should be deemed applicable to the Masonic fraternity.

Mackey asks:

> Look at its ancient landmarks, its sublime ceremonies, its profound symbols and allegories — all inculcating religious observance, and teaching religious truth, and who can deny that it is eminently a religious institution? . . . Masonry, then, is indeed a religious institution; and on this ground mainly, if not alone, should the religious Mason defend it.[7]

We should not be disturbed by the frequent denials of the religious character of the lodge offered by ordinary members. They either do not understand Masonry or they do not know what constitutes a religion. Many other cults are as insistent on denying their religious nature. Jehovah's Witnesses have railed against "religion" for decades and flatly deny that their eschatological sect resembles religion in any form. A faith healing cult such as the

---

[7] *Ibid.,* p. 619.

Unity School of Christianity and an occult mail order sect such as the Rosicrucians also have their reasons for rejecting the name "religion" although they must be so classified by anyone working in the field of religious sociology or comparative religion. If Freemasonry were to acknowledge its religious status, it would compromise the position of thousands of Christian Masons and Protestant ministers who wear the apron.

The Masonic strategy is simple enough. First deny that Masonry is a religion and then proceed to prove that it is. For example, the same Pike who told us "Masonry is not a religion" also tells us, "Every Masonic Lodge is a temple of religion; and its teachings are instruction in religion."[8] What religion? Not Christianity or Judaism or Islam. Rather Freemasonry is a religion which simply demands belief in God and immortality and inculcates a natural morality of salvation by character.

Pike explains:

> Masonry, around whose altars the Christian, the Hebrew, the Moslem, the Brahmin, the followers of Confucius and Zoroaster, can assemble as brethren and unite in prayer to the one God who is above all Baalim, must needs leave to each of its Initiates to look for the foundation of his faith and hope to the written scriptures of his own religion. For itself it finds those truths definite enough, which are written by the finger of God upon the heart of man and on the pages of the book of nature.[9]

In other words "for itself" Masonry considers the doctrines of Christianity quite peripheral and quite unnecessary but if her initiates must look for other sources of religious authority the lodge will not object. At no time, however, does the lodge ever suggest that the religion and morality of the lodge be supplemented by the Church nor does it direct its initiates to the Church. In fact, those who wish to bypass the Church and find their spiritual sustenance in Masonry alone are welcome to do so and, to be candid about it, are much wiser than their brethren who accept the dross and barnacles of Christianity. For many indeed the lodge is church enough and they may testify that they find Freemasonry a

---

[8] Albert Pike, *Morals and Dogma*, p. 213.
[9] *Ibid.*, p. 226.

completely satisfying spiritual home. Those who desert the Christian
church for the lodge would receive the commendation of the
Masonic writer Sir John Cockburn who said, "Creeds arise, have
their day and pass, but Masonry remains. It is built on the rock
of truth, not on the shifting sands of superstition." Obviously those
who have chosen the solid truth of the lodge over the superstition
and sectarian dogmas of the Church have chosen the better part.

Would the searcher for a religious home find all the elements of
a religion in the Masonic lodge? Unquestionably, he would.

He would worship the Grand Architect of the Universe in a
Temple whose lodge room features two chief articles of worship,
an altar and a Volume of Sacred Law, usually but not necessarily
the Holy Bible. Surely, if Masonry were nothing but a mutual
benefit society, it would have no need for an altar. We find no
altars in the board room of the Metropolitan Life Insurance Company or in the lobby of the American Red Cross headquarters.
Mackey tells us:

> From all this we see that the altar in Masonry is not merely a
> convenient article of furniture, intended, like a table, to hold a
> Bible. It is a sacred utensil of religion, intended, like the altars of
> the ancient temples, for religious uses, and thus identifying Masonry,
> by its necessary existence in our Lodges, as a religious institution. Its
> presence should also lead the contemplative Mason to view the
> ceremonies in which it is employed with solemn reverence, as being
> part of a really religious worship.[10]

Like most other paraphernalia in the lodge room the Bible
assumes a symbolic meaning, in this case the scriptures of the
majority of the brethren. It is clear that the Craft recognizes no
particular inspiration of the Bible and places it on a par with the
scriptures of all other religions. Pike explains:

> The Bible is an indispensable part of the furniture of a Christian
> lodge, only because it is the sacred book of the Christian religion.
> The Hebrew Pentateuch in a Hebrew lodge, and the Koran in a
> Mohammedan one, belong on the Altar; and one of these, and the
> Square and Compass, properly understood, are the Great Lights by
> which a Mason must walk and work.[11]

---

[10] Albert G. Mackey, *Encyclopedia of Freemasonry*, p. 60.
[11] Albert Pike, *Morals and Dogma*, p. 11.

George Wingate Chase is even more explicit:

> The Jews, the Chinese, the Turks, each reject, either the New Testament or the Old, or both, and yet we see no good reason why they should not be made Masons. In fact Blue Lodge Masonry has nothing whatever to do with the Bible; it is not founded upon the Bible. If it was it would not be Masonry; it would be something else.[12]

The Bible in the lodge room is not a standard of religious belief but a symbol of a religious attitude toward life. The central allegory of Freemasonry, the assassination of Hiram Abiff, is nowhere recorded in the Bible. The lodge usually picks passages from the Bible for its liturgy which do not mention Christ lest His name scandalize non-Christian Masons.

Our religious inquirer would know that each candidate for the lodge, in Anglo-Saxon jurisdictions, must affirm belief in a Supreme Architect and in immortality. The shock of entrance of the first degree serves as his Masonic baptism or rebirth as he moves from self-acknowledged darkness and helplessness into the light of Masonic teaching. Mackey describes the shock of entrance in the following words:

> There he stands without our portals, on the threshhold of this new Masonic life, in darkness, helplessness, and ignorance. Having been wandering amid the errors and covered over with the pollutions of the outer and profane world, he comes inquiringly to our doors, seeking the new birth, and asking a withdrawal of the veil which conceals divine truth from his uninitiated sight. . . . There is to be, not simply a change for the future, but also an extinction of the past; for initiation is, as it were, a death to the world and a resurrection to a new life. . . . The world is left behind — the chains of error and ignorance which had previously restrained the candidate in moral and intellectual captivity are broken — the portals of the Temple have been thrown widely open, and Masonry stands before the neophyte in all the glory of its form and beauty, to be fully revealed to him, however, only when the new birth has been completely accomplished.[13]

Masonry makes no references to that baptism which makes the Christian a participant in God's own life, to the sacraments of the Church, to the revealed truths of the gospel. All men alike come to

---

[12] George Wingate Chase, *Digest of Masonic Law*, p. 207.
[13] Albert G. Mackey, *Masonic Ritualist*, p. 23.

the portals of the Masonic Temple ignorant of divine truths and aimless wanderers.

The Masonic initiate knows that:

> A Lodge is said to be opened in the name of God and the Holy Saints John, as a declaration of the sacred and religious purposes of our meetings, of our profound reverence for that Divine Being whose name and attributes should be the constant theme of our contemplation, and of our respect for those ancient patrons whom the traditions of Masonry have so intimately connected with the history of the institution.[14]

During the degree workings the initiate has bound himself by solemn oaths taken on the V.S.L. and asked God Himself to witness his resolve to keep the secrets of the order and to enter into specific relationships with his new brethren. All the ritual, prayers, hymns, candles, and vestments of a liturgical church are his in the Temple.

The Craft also furnishes him with a moral code which makes no reference to other religions or to models of conduct except that of the Masonic hero: Hiram Abiff. At no time is the Christian Mason encouraged to pattern his life after his Saviour or to cultivate the specifically Christian virtues. This Masonic morality is selective. In regulating his sex life he may remember his Masonic oath: "I promise and swear that I will not violate the chastity of a Mason's wife, his mother, sister or daughter, knowing them to be such." Presumably all others are fair game and such seductions and rapes in no way violate his obligation. We need not speculate on the public reaction to such a moral code if publicly advanced by a Christian denomination.

His Masonic mentors assure him that fidelity to the principles of the lodge will win him entry to "Thy lodge on high." In explaining the term "Acacian" Mackey explains that this refers to "A Mason who by living in strict accord with his obligations is free from sin."[15] The Mason wins salvation not through the passion and death of Jesus Christ but through the mythical assassination of Hiram Abiff.

---

[14] *Ibid.*, p. 14.
[15] Albert G. Mackey, *Masonic Lexicon*, p. 16.

He knows that when he dies he will be clothed in the Masonic apron and buried by his brethren. They will assure his survivors that if he has lived according to Masonic principles he will enjoy the bliss of heaven. After the religious services, if any, the lodge takes charge of the graveside ceremony. The assembled brethren sing the following funeral dirge written in 1816:

Solemn strikes the funeral chime,
Notes of our departing time;
As we journey here below
Through a pilgrimage of woe.

Mortals, now indulge a tear,
For mortality is here!
See how wide her trophies wave
O'er the slumbers of the grave.

Here another guest we bring!
Seraphs of celestial wing,
To our fun'ral altar come,
Waft a friend and brother home.

Lord of all, below, above,
Fill our souls with truth and love;
As dissolves our earthly tie,
Take us to Thy lodge on high.

Perhaps during his lifetime he had the opportunity to witness the consecrating and constituting of a new lodge. This ceremony with its obvious religious character is described by the English Masonic historian Jones:

The Consecrating Officer, acting on behalf of the Grand Master, opens a lodge in three degrees, and, to the accompaniment of suitable prayers, scripture readings, and addresses, uncovers the lodge board and scatters corn (the symbol of plenty), pours wine (the symbol of joy and cheerfulness), pours oil (the symbol of peace and unanimity), and sprinkles salt (the symbol of fidelity and friendship). He then dedicates the lodge, and the Chaplain takes the censer three times round the lodge and offers the prayer of dedication. The Consecrating Officer then officially consecrates the lodge, and there generally follows the installation of the first Master, the election and appointment of officers, the approval of bylaws, etc., etc. In the old rites, still followed under some of the American jurisdictions, there is placed upon a table in front of the Consecrating Officer an emblem known as the "lodge" — an oblong box of white fabric, to hold the warrant and the constitutions — and round it are placed three candles and the vessels containing the consecrating elements.[16]

Masonry meets all the essential requirements of a religion. It is not Christianity but it is religion. Mackey states:

> Speculative Masonry, now known as Freemasonry, is, therefore, the scientific application and the religious consecration of the rules and principles, the technical language and the implements and materials, of operative Masonry to the worship of God as the Grand Architect of the Universe, and to the purification of the heart and the inculcation of the dogmas of a religious philosophy.[17]

Man arrives at an understanding of this religious philosophy through reason alone, says Masonry. Consequently, this religion of naturalism never rises above the level of any of the non-Christian "higher" religions. For some a blending of Masonry and their own religion may be a possibility; such a course is not open to the Christian.

Nowhere in Masonry is it suggested that a man be born again in baptism, that God became man in Jesus Christ, that He died for man's sins, that He founded a Church with authority to teach what is necessary for salvation. These become secondary, supplementary, and "sectarian" dogmas in the eyes of the lodge. Under no circumstances should they violate Masonic etiquette by dragging these dogmas into the lodge or mention the name of Jesus Christ aloud among their brethren. This is the real apostasy of the Christian Mason. Here is where the Christian Mason assumes the role of Peter on the night of the crucifixion. While he stands in the lodge among those who deny and ignore Christ and participates in worship and prayer from which his Redeemer's name is carefully excluded he is testifying before men: "I know not the man."

The lodge has tried to eliminate the slightest reference to Christianity in its rituals and monitors. Mackey remarks:

> The Blazing Star is said, by Webb, to be "commemorative of the star which appeared to guide the wise men of the East to the place of our Saviour's nativity." This, which is one of the ancient interpretations of the symbols, being considered too sectarian in its character,

---

[16] Bernard E. Jones, *Freemasons' Guide and Compendium*, p. 347.
[17] Albert G. Mackey, *Masonic Ritualist*, p. 75.

and unsuitable to the universal religion of Masonry, has been omitted since the meeting of Grand Lecturers at Baltimore, in 1842.[18]

Christ has told the Christian Mason "No man cometh to the Father, but by me," but the Mason supports the lodge which promises eternal happiness to all who live by Masonic principles. He stands at the grave of an unbaptized brother and answers "So mote it be" to the Worshipful Master's assurance that the deceased has attained "Thy lodge on high." He knows he has been commanded by Christ to go and teach all nations and yet he submits to a gag on religious discussion in a religious organization dedicated to the worship of God.

This dilemma does not face the Catholic since he knows that his Church has exposed the religious pretensions of the lodge for more than two centuries. Many Protestants and Eastern Orthodox also belong to denominations which forbid any compromise with the lodge. Furthermore, this choice between Church and lodge does not face modernist Protestants, Unitarians, and Jews who deny the exclusive claims of the Christian faith, doubt or deny the divinity of Jesus Christ, dismiss the inspiration of the Bible.

The problem of dual membership in lodge and Church weighs heaviest on those evangelical Protestants, particularly ministers, who attempt to combine the religious tenets of Christianity with those of Masonic naturalism, who try to serve Hiram Abiff and Jesus Christ on alternate evenings. As the Lutheran writer, the Rev. Theodore Graebner, put it: "The difficulty for a Christian remaining a Freemason, then, consists in this, that Christ is not satisfied to share His homage with Allah and with Buddha."[19]

In practically every respect Masonry resembles the mystery religions and as such represents not Christianity but a return to paganism. Mackey points out that Masonry "is not Christianity, but there is nothing repugnant to the faith of a Christian."[20] But this is the point: Masonry is admittedly and obviously religious but it is not Christianity and this in itself is repugnant to the faith of a Christian.

---

[18] *Ibid.*, p. 56.
[19] Theodore Graebner, *Is Masonry a Religion?*, p. 60.
[20] Albert G. Mackey, *Encyclopedia of Freemasonry*, p. 641.

CHAPTER VI

THE MASONIC OATHS

Do They Meet Requirements for a Valid Extrajudicial Oath?

Christians have always regarded an oath, the calling upon God to witness the truth of a statement, as a most serious act of religion. In fact, some Christians, such as the Quakers and the Mennonites, following a literal interpretation of Christ's injunction "not to swear at all" (Mt. 5:33–37), refuse to swear any oath even in a court of law. Catholics and the majority of other Christians do not interpret this scriptural passage as an absolute prohibition against oaths but as an ideal to be realized in a Christian society where oaths would be unnecessary. Nevertheless moral theologians emphasize the gravity of an oath and insist that certain conditions be met before a Christian may swear an oath without being guilty of taking the name of the Lord in vain.

For failure to meet these conditions in the Masonic lodge the Church objects to the solemn obligations or oaths exacted from the candidate for the Blue Lodge degrees. We have described the Blue Lodge initiations in Chapter III and have given the three oaths of Entered Apprentice (p. 28), Fellow Craft (p. 35), and Master Mason (p. 40). We will not repeat these oaths but invite the reader to refresh his memory by reviewing them as presented in context. Nor will we examine the many oaths in the

Scottish and York rites since these rites do not form an integral part of pure and ancient Masonry.

The Christian objection to the Shriner's obligation taken "upon this Bible" and on the mysterious legend of the Koran and its dedication to the Mohammedan faith (p. 112) is obvious to all but the most insensitive. The Shriner gives his oath "upon this sacred book, by the sincerity of a Moslem's oath" and concludes by beseeching "Allah, the god of Arab Moslem and Mohammedan, the god of our fathers, support me to the entire fulfillment of the same. Amen. Amen. Amen." A few Protestant Masons have attempted to defend the Blue Lodge oaths as permissible but, to my knowledge, no one has risked his theological reputation by trying to justify the oath of the Mystic Shrine.

The chief objection of the Church to the Masonic oath is that it fails to meet the essential requirement for a valid extrajudicial oath, namely, that the matter of the oath be of a serious nature. To call upon the Almighty to witness an oath concerning some trifle is to take the name of God in vain. Actually what the Masonic candidate swears to conceal is nothing more than a few passwords, secret grips, and lodge rites. To call upon God to witness such a promise indicates a lack of respect and an abuse of the virtue of religion.

Masonry may be entitled to preserve harmless secrets in order to heighten the interest of prospective members and amuse the brethren. It may employ passwords to exclude the merely curious from its assemblies. But to suggest that the oaths demanded of the candidate are needed to protect such secrets is ridiculous. A gentleman's promise would serve as well and this is all that other "secret societies" such as the Knights of Columbus expect.

A family may keep certain secrets within the family circle but can we imagine the father gathering his children around the family altar, blindfolding them, and asking them to place their hands on the Holy Bible and to declare that they would rather have their toes split one by one, their hair pulled out by the roots, and their legs tied in a bow knot rather than reveal that the front door key is usually kept under the door mat?

We can have no doubt that the Masonic oaths are meant to be solemn and binding in a religious sense. The candidate takes them in a lodge opened in the name of God and the Holy Saints John. He takes them kneeling before the altar of Masonry with his hands on an open Bible and seals the oath by kissing the Bible. In fact, he does everything but sign his name with his own blood. Not even in a courtroom where he is asked to take an oath as a witness is he asked to demonstrate his sincerity to a greater degree than in the lodge room.

We can see that the Entered Apprentice oath pertains mainly to secrecy, while the second and third involve obligations toward his brethren in the lodge. The candidate freely consents to the most horrible mutilations and punishments should he ever reveal any of the secrets of the lodge. By the time he has become a full fledged Master Mason he has agreed to have his throat cut, tongue torn out by the roots, his body buried in the sands of the sea, his breast torn open, his heart plucked out and devoured by vultures, his body sliced in two, his bowels removed and burned to ashes and the ashes scattered to the four winds should he ever violate so much as one iota of his obligation. He emphasizes, "All this I solemnly swear . . . without any hesitation, mental reservation, or secret evasion of mind whatever . . ."

Hannah poses the basic dilemma of the Masonic oaths when he writes, "Either the oaths mean what they say, or they do not. If they do mean what they say, then the candidate is entering into a pact consenting to his own murder by barbarous torture and mutilation should he break it. If they do not mean what they say, then he is swearing high-sounding schoolboy nonsense on the Bible, which verges on blasphemy."[1]

Of course, the standard Masonic rejoinder is that although the pledge to secrecy is to be observed absolutely the punishments themselves are to be understood in a symbolic sense. And yet the candidate has declared that he is swearing the oaths "without hesitation, mental reservation, or secret evasion of mind," and it would seem to most people that to understand these mutilations

---

[1] Walton Hannah, Darkness Visible (London: Augustine Press, 1952), p. 21.

and murder as symbolic is not the plain meaning of the text. Further, even the symbolic sense is quite contrary to the laws of the land which do not tolerate murder or mutilation for disclosing a password. If these are the symbolic punishments for disclosing a password, what are the symbolic punishments for treason and grand larceny and rape?

"But you are taking this whole business of the oath too seriously," sigh the Masonic defenders. And this is the whole point: a Christian cannot study the New Testament and come to any conclusion but that only a serious reason will force him to swear an oath. Not only are the secrets of Masonry trivial by nature but they are common knowledge among those who take the time and trouble to investigate them. For a dollar or two the curious may purchase Masonic rituals from bookstores, the National Christian Association, and Masonic publishing houses.

This brings up the interesting point that almost every past and present lodge officer has violated his Entered Apprentice oath wherein he pledged that he would not "print, paint, stamp, stain, cut, carve, mark, or engrave them (the arts, parts or points of Ancient Free Masonry), or cause the same to be done, on anything movable or immovable, capable of receiving the least impression of a word, syllable, letter, or character, whereby the same may become legible or intelligible to any person under the canopy of heaven, and the secrets of Masonry thereby unlawfully obtained through my unworthiness." In order to conduct the lengthy Masonic initiations and to memorize their respective parts the officers are obliged to purchase and study copies of *Ecce Orienti* or *King Solomon's Temple*, or such rituals as Duncan's and Ronayne which are furnished by Masonic supply houses. In so doing they would at least be accessories to the crime.

The triviality of the matter of the Masonic oath is not the sole objection which the Church raises. She also declares the oath immoral in that it binds the candidate in uncertain things. Like King Herod, the candidate gives his solemn word in things which are hidden to him. Herod discovered that Salome wanted the head of St. John the Baptist and the Masonic candidate may find out that he has entered a mystery cult which denies any place to his Saviour, which practices a death and resurrection rite in the third degree, and which makes demands he is not able to meet.

The Bible speaks of just such oaths and points out that it does not matter whether the thing involved is good or evil: "The person that sweareth, and uttereth with his lips, that he would do either evil or good, and bindeth the same with an oath, and his word: and having forgotten it afterwards understandeth his offence. Let him do penance for his sin . . ." (Lev. 5:4–5).

Finally, we must state that Masonry has no right to impose an oath on its initiates. That right is reserved to the Church and to legitimate civil authorities. The lodge has no more right to administer such an oath than the Mau Mau or the Chinese tongs. Nor has the lodge any right to keep secrets from legitimate authority in the political or spiritual areas.

The Masonic oaths are taken under false pretenses and are therefore null and void. The Master assures the candidate that nothing in the oath will interfere with "the duty you owe to your God, your neighbor, your country, or self." But the Christian knows that "No one cometh to the Father, but by me" and that in worship he must honor the Son of God, Jesus Christ, who is ignored by lodge religion. He may indeed belong to a Christian denomination which forbids lodge affiliation and by accepting initiation he is severing his church affiliation. Of what value then are the Worshipful Master's assurances? When the candidate realizes that his oath has interfered with his duties toward God he need not consider the oath binding in conscience.

How inconsistent would be the Church to expend energies organizing Holy Name Societies among Catholic men, devoting sermons and pamphlets to the evils of taking the name of the Lord in vain, reciting the divine praises in reparation for sins of blasphemy, while at the same time allowing her sons to participate in solemn religious rites centering around oaths to conceal the passwords "Boaz" and "Shibboleth" and "Tubal Cain" and a few knuckle jabs and lodge ceremonies!

At least the Grand Orients do not fall under the condemnation

of the Church because of their oaths. They reject a belief in God
and simply ask the candidate to promise on the Constitutions of
the lodge.

Christians of all denominations know that "Thou shalt not take
the name of the Lord in vain." They will consent to swear an oath
in court and under certain other circumstances but they know that
a sacred oath is not a suitable stage prop for a lodge initiation.
Because the Masonic oath violates the conditions for a valid extrajudicial oath the Church must condemn the oath and the sect which
imposes it.

CHAPTER VII

ANTI-CATHOLICISM IN AMERICAN LODGES

Scottish Rite Spearheads Attack on the Church

Some Catholics seem to believe that the local Masonic lodges wage an incessant campaign of calumny and slander against Catholicism which accounts for the adamant stand of the Church on the lodge question. On the contrary, we find that the only actively hostile propaganda originates in one quasi-Masonic body, the Southern Jurisdiction of the Scottish rite with headquarters in the nation's capital.

The Blue Lodges generally adhere to the Masonic landmark which forbids discussion of religion and politics in the lodge. A Master Mason who would confide that he has never heard a word against Catholicism or any other Christian denomination in his Mother Lodge may be quite sincere. He may even deplore the frankly anti-clerical activities of his Latin brethren in the Grand Orients or the similar activities of the so-called "higher degrees" which do not hold themselves bound by the same ground rules as pure and ancient Masonry.

Specific violations of this Masonic gag on religious discussion may be reported but we believe it is only fair to say that this prohibition is scrupulously observed in most American lodges. Anson Phelps Stokes quotes an anonymous but highly placed American Mason on the question of Freemasonry and Catholicism:

I do not think symbolic or Blue Lodge Masonry as a whole is anti-Catholic anywhere in this country. I do think that many Masons are anti-Catholic either from personal prejudice or because they are misled by anti-Masonic feeling among Catholics to believe that Masonry should have the same sort of feeling toward the Church of Rome. The Southern Jurisdiction of the Ancient and Accepted Scottish Rite of course has been for a long time very definitely anti-Catholic, both in its political activities against parochial schools, public transportation furnished by the State to private schools, and otherwise. I know of no Grand Lodge in this country which either itself pursues or permits among its Lodges any anti-Catholic activities. Freemasonry, of course, is in no way responsible for radical writers in the anti-Catholic press who choose to attempt to hitch up Masonry with their particular variety of propaganda.[1]

Animated by the crude bigotry of Pike and the modernized nativism of Paul Blanshard, the Southern Scottish rite continues to disseminate a vicious brand of anti-Catholicism among its nearly half million members. Its *New Age* magazine which goes to the homes of all Scottish rite Masons in 33 Southern and Western states every month, supplies a steady diet of inflammatory material designed to arouse suspicion, ridicule, and hatred of the Church in this country and abroad. Scottish rite members in the companion Northern Jurisdiction, Knights Templar, and the bulk of Masons who never go beyond the third degree may have only the faintest notion of the type of diatribes to which these other Scottish rite Masons are subjected, month in and month out. Although practically every Mason knows of the antagonism between Church and Craft, he is often genuinely shocked to discover the editorial depths to which the *New Age* sinks.

It happens, however, that the general public may subscribe to this magazine or may consult back issues in any large library. A dip into the *New Age* itself should convince the most skeptical Mason that the Scottish rite, Southern Jurisdiction, is waging a full-scale war on Catholicism, parochial and private schools, and any venture of the Christian church into the area of public morals. Any assortment of back issues will prove this assertion; for our purposes

---

[1] Anson Phelps Stokes, *Church and State in the United States* (New York: Harper & Brothers, 1950), pp. 252–253.

we have chosen the six issues of the *New Age* from January to June, 1957, inclusive.

Each issue carries on the back cover a list of five points favored by the Supreme Council 33°. The first point of this platform recommends the American public schools "for all the children of all the people." From 1920 to 1939 the magazine expressed this educational policy in the following words: "We approve and reassert our belief in the free and compulsory education of the children of our nation in public primary schools supported by public taxation." Point two urges the inculcation of patriotism, respect for law and order and loyalty to the Constitution. Point three in the current statement asks for compulsory use of English in instruction in all public grammar schools. The fourth point recommends that adequate provision be made in the public schools for the education of "alien populations" in the principles of American institutions and citizenship. Finally, in point five the Supreme Council advocates "entire separation of Church and State, and opposition to every attempt to appropriate public moneys — federal, state, or local — directly or indirectly, for the support of sectarian or private institutions."

Immediately below this statement of principles appears the following statement whose irony will become apparent to those who examine the contents of the magazine: "This Supreme Council neither makes nor permits to be made in its publications any criticism of any religious faith or church."

Furthermore the editors attempt to disclaim responsibility for most of what appears in the pages of the *New Age* by prefacing their editorial comments with: "The editorials published in the *New Age* are written by special writers and . . . are unofficial in character and represent the views of the writers, not necessarily the composite views of the Supreme Council." The *New Age* is probably the only *official* publication of any association in the country which refuses to stand behind its own editorials. The magazine also includes two notices in each issue warning anyone against reprinting the contents without permission.

Considerable space is devoted in the *New Age* to eulogizing the public schools at the expense of private educational systems. The

Scottish rite assumes a proprietary role over the public schools; no one need look in the pages of the New Age for serious attempts to investigate the implications of a pluralist society in the area of education. An editorial on page 6 of the January issue describes the plight of certain Protestant students at Bradfordsville, Ky., a predominantly Catholic community, who must travel eight or ten miles to attend a public high school while a local Catholic school allegedly receives support from public coffers. A few pages later the editorial writer blasts released time education programs. On page 9 the writer repeats charges that Catholic priests incited mobs to violence in South America in an editorial entitled "Murder in Colombia." The Scottish rite even objects to consideration of Catholic petitions for financial assistance for their schools by the government of New Zealand. This editorial on page 11 concludes with the charge that Catholic schools are "primarily instruments for proselyting and the spread of Vatican propaganda," and therefore should not be supported from "the public treasury of any nation that values either its integrity or its safety." The next editorial approvingly quotes Dr. Eugene Carson Blake who had advocated an end to tax exemption for church property in a Reformation Sunday sermon in Cincinnati. The Masonic commentator maintains that title to Catholic Church property rests not with the congregation, pastor or bishop but with the Vatican, "a foreign political entity" consistently and avowedly the enemy of our Constitution and Bill of Rights. Finally, in this same issue the editorial writer objects to a statement attributed to Vice-President Nixon that the Catholic Church is "one of the major bulwarks against communism and totalitarian ideas."

A partial explanation for this preoccupation with Catholicism might be suggested if the New Age were simply defending Masonry against the daily attacks of the Roman Church. The Church reaches her millions of faithful through hundreds of magazines and newspapers in this country alone and if this communications network is conducting a concerted attack on the lodge we may perhaps excuse the New Age's obsession. But we may get some idea of the one sided nature of this dialogue by consulting the Catholic

Periodical Index. This index lists all the articles by subject matter which appear in more than 100 Catholic periodicals including the leading American and foreign journals. If the Church is carrying on an attack on the Craft comparable to that which the *New Age* is waging on the Church we would expect to see this reflected in the index. We find that in the four year period from 1952 to 1956 a total of nine editorials or articles relating to Masonry appeared in English-language Catholic periodicals listed in the *Periodical Index.* A single issue of a single Masonic magazine such as the *New Age* may carry more than the total output of English-language Catholic magazines for a year or more.

The February, 1957, issue of the *New Age* is typical. On page 71 the editorialist declares: "One of the foulest and most pernicious of the pressure groups that infests the world of international politics today is the Roman Church hierarchy and its several instrumentalities." He goes on to say that no political group has done more to "injure the cause of freedom" or cause dissension among peoples. He brands the hierarchy as "self-seeking" and utterly lacking in moral "scruples." Please remember that the writer is not discussing international Communism but the oldest and by far the largest body of Christians in the world.

An editorial entitled "Morals and Advertising" attacks the newspaper advertisements sponsored by the Knights of Columbus as "calculated to deceive the readers," and as being against "every commonly accepted standard of moral worth." The writer castigates them as "evasion, distortions, half-truths and whole fabrications," and equates them in "brazen lack of regard for the truth" with the motion picture ads complained of by the Legion of Decency (page 74).

A lengthy article on pages 91–96 entitled "Conflict Between the Popes and Freemasonry" ridicules the idea that Masonry wishes to destroy the Catholic Church and expresses disbelief that any Catholic except in "backward countries like Spain and Colombia" would swallow such a canard. Catholic readers of the *New Age* might also be understandably misled into thinking that the lodge wishes ill of the Church. In fact if the Catholic Church were as vile an institution as the articles in the *New Age* indicate, the lodge could have no other course than to work for its destruction.

"The Need for Synthesis," an article which appears on pages 100–102, questions the moral right of Roman Catholics to serve on school boards or teach in public schools if they agree with the educational policies of their Church. The author urges that young people choose their political party and their Church when they reach maturity. They can make this choice wisely, he explains, by attending schools "protected by the people from political and ecclesiastical interference." The concern that all American children attend the public schools has, it must be noted, never led the *New Age* to advocate racial integration of the public schools; the racial exclusiveness of Masonry and of the Scottish rite itself is one of the chief extralegal supports of the system of segregation which characterizes the social pattern of certain Southern states.

In the March issue, page 134, the editorialist rehashes the flurry over the cancellation of the film *Martin Luther* by a Chicago T.V. station. The Chancery of the archdiocese emphasized that it had no objection to the showing but upheld the democratic right of those who protested as well. This did not assuage the *New Age* which assured its readers that any declaration by the Roman hierarchy that no pressure was used is clearly false. The next editorial applauds a decision of the Pennsylvania supreme court which denied the right of pupils at a Catholic school to ride a tax-supported school bus. The *New Age* declared that any policy which would allow public funds to transport pupils to a nonpublic school would be "foolish."

The third editorial in the March issue questions the sincerity of the bishops of Quebec who spoke out against alcoholism. The Masonic writer felt compelled to point out that the Church could not really favor temperance since for centuries abbeys and monasteries had been manufacturing liquors such as Chartreuse and Benedictine (page 137). The final editorial in this issue concludes, by charging the Church with having been "a gigantic force for evil in world politics for fifteen centuries. . . ." But as we know, the New Age does not tolerate criticism of "any religious faith or church."

A feature article entitled "A Challenge to Scottish Rite Masons" (pages 143–145) worries about the attitudes of men in government regarding "separation of church and state" and "nonpartisan democratic education." The writer urges that Masonic bodies encourage Masons and children of Masons to seek federal employment.

The lead editorial in the April issue accuses the Catholic authorities of Augusta, Maine, of blackmailing the city to provide bus transportation for 900 parochial school pupils. The writer rejoices that some Catholic children might be forced to switch to the public schools for lack of transportation: "It will be a salutary experience for them to go to a real American school, many of them for the first time in their lives (page 198)." On pages 203–204 the New Age commends the POAU objection to Jesuit ownership of radio and TV stations in this country. The author of "The Rising Tide," a 33rd degree Mason, upholds the present national origins immigration act and notes that the hierarchy and "groups listed as subversive" are doing everything possible to secure greater immigration from southern Europe, especially from Italy, "the greatest stronghold of Communism in Europe aside from the Soviet Union (page 217)."

An unsigned article entitled "Supreme Court Appointee Questioned" on pages 223–224 discusses the questions relative to his religion which were put to Supreme Court Justice William J. Brennan. It maintains that Brennan and other Catholic officials, "because of this apparent demand for blind obedience to Papal doctrine," ought to be examined further on "their attitude toward the pronouncements of Pius XII," and on how they may solve "the conflict between their oath of office and their religious obligation." We wonder if 32nd degree Masons should be similarly questioned on their lodge obligations and whether or not they agree with the New Age's demand for a religious test for officeholders.

The Newman Club apostolate on secular campuses is discussed with the magazine's typical candor in the June issue. An editorial called "Assault on Our Universities," warns against the "infiltration of Romanism into our nonsectarian or secular cultural centers," comparing it to Communism. It concludes with the charge that for the Catholic clergy the end justifies the means, even the most evil (page 329). We are told that the clergy freely use "sophistry, distortion, innuendo, and outright falsehood" to advance their aims. We speculate on what more the writer might have added in the order of invective had the New Age tolerated "any criticism of any religious faith or church," but we are assured by the statement on the back cover of every issue that such criticism would not be tolerated.

We believe that any impartial observer must agree that these sample passages from six recent consecutive issues of the official organ of the Scottish rite, Southern Jurisdiction, fully demonstrate the animosity of that Masonic body to Catholicism. Anyone can verify these passages by checking the back issues of the magazine in a library; anyone can take a much wider sampling of the New Age to satisfy himself that these six issues are representative; anyone is also free to speculate that if these are the printed sentiments of the Supreme Council, then the inner and secret deliberations and machinations reflect the same bias.

The inside back cover of each issue presents a complete list of the pamphlets and books sold by the Supreme Council. The titles include The Double Doctrine of the Church of Rome by Von Zedtwitz, Humanum Genus — Pope of Rome's Letter Against Freemasonry and Albert Pike's Reply, and The Truth Shall Make You Free — the Pope's Letter Attacking the Public School System and the Supreme Council's Resolutions Relative to Same. Members can also order Pike's Hymns to the Gods and Other Poems and his Indo-Aryan Deities and Worship as Contained in the Rig-Veda; Interpretations of the Deities of the Veda and of the Real Meaning of the Veda.

In its August issue (1957), the New Age urges the support of all non-Catholics for a shelter for renegade Catholic priests at Sea Cliff, N. Y. This center, sponsored by Christ's Mission, plans to offer rehabilitation and guidance to priests who have been freed "from the slavery the Roman church demands." The Scottish rite repeatedly endorses the work of Christ's Mission which is staffed by ex-priests and ex-religious and publishes the vicious *Converted Catholic* magazine whose venom surpasses that of the *New Age* itself. The rite also claims a large share of the credit for the founding of Protestants and Other Americans United for Separation of Church and State, or simply POAU. It furnishes part of the annual budget of POAU which warns Americans of the Roman menace to free institutions and traditions.

When a Franciscan priest in Arizona left the priesthood and wrote a bitter autobiography he revealed the solicitude of the Masonic order for apostate Catholic priests. Such unfortunate men are lionized by Masonic writers and helped to establish themselves in other professions. This particular priest admits that when he foresaw his eventual defection he took the precaution of getting a majority of Masons on the board of the private hospital which he was operating.[1] Later when another apostate priest came to him for help he referred him to "Masonic friends" on the West Coast.[2] The woman with whom he attempted marriage was the daughter of a Mason. Another former priest, now a 32nd degree Mason, pens an occasional article for the *New Age*.

Masonic opposition to parochial schools, whether Catholic or Protestant, is clear cut. The lodge and the Ku Klux Klan supported referendums commanding attendance at public schools in Oregon, California, and Michigan. The referendum was defeated in the latter two states and reversed by the U. S. Supreme Court in Oregon. Presently, the rite is attempting to remove the tax exemption for parochial and private schools in California. This exemption was upheld by the California Supreme Court in 1956 but the Sovereign Grand Inspector General for the state organized an appeal to the U. S. Supreme Court which in turn refused to accept jurisdiction over the California court. California voters defeated the proposition to lift the tax exemption in the 1958 election by a two to one margin.

---

[1] Emmett McLoughlin, *People's Padre* (Boston: Beacon, 1954), p. 116.
[2] *Ibid.*, p. 237.

Fr. Mark Hurley in the March, 1960, issue of *Information* magazine reported: "A new law which required the reporting of campaign contributions unveiled the identity of the opposition. It revealed that contributions of over $250,000 had been raised not only by California Masonic lodges but by Masonic bodies in 34 states, Puerto Rico, Alaska and the Canal Zone. These facts were not widely published" (p. 28).

We need not imagine that all Scottish rite Masons look to the *New Age* for direction or even bother to read it. One of the pet peeves of the magazine has been the proposal for an accredited United States representative at the Vatican. The editors are convinced that this is the top priority objective of the American hierarchy and that Catholics are itching to maneuver such an appointment. During World War II President Roosevelt appointed Myron Taylor as his personal representative to the Holy See and later President Truman proposed sending Gen. Mark Clark on a similar mission. Oddly enough, however, the four principals in the cast of characters of this "Catholic" plot carried undisputed Masonic credentials — all were 32nd or 33rd degree Masons of the Scottish rite.

Intelligent Masons, including many of those exposed to the monthly vituperations of the *New Age*, discount the crude anti-Catholicism and nativism of the Southern Scottish rite just as they discount the racism and paganism of Pike. They regret the alliance between the rite and the KKK in Oregon and in some Southern states. They realize that a state monopoly of education is fraught with dangers and they acknowledge the basic right of parochial and private schools to exist even when they may disagree with the sponsoring agency's religious beliefs.

Scottish rite Masons in the Southern jurisdiction encounter anti-Catholicism not only in the *New Age* but in practically every book published under the rite's auspices. In the book they probably received when they entered the rite they read:

> Now, from the tomb in which after his murders he rotted, Clement the Fifth howls against the successors of his victims, in the Allocutions of Pio Nono against the Freemasons. The ghosts of the dead Templars

haunt the Vatican and disturb the slumbers of the paralyzed Papacy, which, dreading the dead, shrieks out its excommunications and impotent anathemas against the living.[3]

A contemporary Masonic writer denies any Masonic hostility toward the Church on the same page in which he launches a typical attack:

> In free America, there has never been any opposition to Catholicism as a religion so far as Freemasonry is concerned, for the one cardinal principle which the fraternity has contended is that of toleration — the absolute right of every man to worship God in accordance with his own convictions. . . . It is only necessary to review the religious persecutions inspired by the Church of Rome over a period of three hundred years when thousands of people were burned at the stake, massacred at St. Bartholomew, tortured, murdered, persecuted, to realize that all the fulminations which have been uttered against Freemasonry or may be thundered forth in the future are simply the frantic rantings of one of the most pernicious and dogmatic institutions ever born into the world under the guise of religion.[4]

Almost every issue of the monthly *Masonic Inspiration* reveals the fanatical hatred of the editor against the Catholic Church. For example, in the March, 1960, issue the editor seeks to defend the public schools against supposed Catholic attacks. He asks, "Or are the godless schools the ones that have turned out the present crop of Catholic gangsters, racketeers, thieves, wolf-pack killers, Chicago ticket fixers? The Roman Catholic hierarchy, aware of the preponderance of malefactors among their people, is attempting to hide their guilt behind the 'godless school' smoke screen. It's time the American people were awakened to the fact that the real godless schools are the parochial schools that give us all our moral misfits" (p. 2).

The same Masonic editor, Charles Van Cott, proposes in the June, 1960, issue that "The Federal Government should demand that every Knight of Columbus and member of the papal hierarchy go before a Federal judge and be compelled to renounce his allegiance to a foreign potentate and assume an oath of allegiance and loyalty to the Federal constitution and the American flag" (p. 2).

---

[3] Albert Pike, *Morals and Dogma*, p. 815.
[4] Delmar Duane Durrah, *History and Evolution of Freemasonry*, p. 268.

We have already pointed out that the "higher degrees" do not form an integral part of Masonry and, therefore, the obvious anti-Catholicism of the Scottish rite should not be taken to represent the Blue Lodges. Nevertheless the powerful Grand Lodges should not receive complete absolution; they could easily exercise a measure of control over the bigotry of the Southern jurisdiction just as they could lift the bars against Negro members if they wished. After all, membership in the Blue Lodge is a prerequisite of membership in the Scottish and York rites. The Grand Lodge could conceivably excommunicate Masons who affiliate with quasi-Masonic rites which systematically and openly violate the Masonic landmarks of impartiality in religion and politics. Since the Grand Lodges in this country do not protest against the traditional religious baiting of the Scottish rite they must assume a share of the condemnation.

Masons must know that in the public mind the fine distinctions between Blue Lodge, Scottish rite, Knights Templar, and the Shrine are blurred and all but meaningless. Most non-Masons assume that a man enters as a first degree Mason, advances to 32nd or 33rd degree, and finally joins the Shrine, which they are likely to believe is the top Masonic degree. To the uninitiated they are all Masonic bodies and the activities of the "higher degrees" and the various fun orders are all reflections of the Masonic spirit. The layman neither knows nor cares which degrees are "officially" Masonic and which are not. The vaunted Masonic abhorrence of religious debate and political action becomes a sham when he sees the blatant attitude toward religion and politics of the Scottish rite, Southern Jurisdiction.

CHAPTER VIII

PAPAL CONDEMNATIONS OF THE LODGE

*Eight Popes Have Condemned Masonry
Since 1738*

No one could accuse the Catholic Church of disguising her antipathy to Freemasonry. Scarcely 20 years after the organization of modern Masonry in 1717 Pope Clement XII forbade membership in the lodge and since then seven other popes have warned the faithful against the dangers of Masonic naturalism to the Christian faith.

Catholics who join the Masonic sect are automatically excommunicated. Except at the point of death only the pope or his delegated representative can lift this excommunication in the external forum. Such a "Catholic" Mason deprives himself of the spiritual benefits of the Church, may not receive the sacraments, and cannot be given Christian burial nor be interred in consecrated ground. A Mason who desires to enter the Church must cut all ties with the lodge. A Mason who wishes to marry a Catholic woman must reveal his lodge affiliation in signing the pre-nuptial questionnaire.

Excommunication is a drastic penalty but its object is to cure the offenders and bring them back to the Church. Obviously a non-Catholic cannot be excluded from the communion of the faithful to which he does not belong. Masonic jibing at the ineffectiveness of papal excommunication for Protestant and Jewish Masons betrays a complete misunderstanding of the term. The Church does not excommunicate Masons. She excommunicates Catholics who freely elect to worship the Grand Architect of the lodge rather than the Father, Son, and Holy Spirit.

In previous chapters we have examined the chief reasons for the Church's severe attitude toward Masonry. Masonry constitutes a religion of naturalism which considers the basic Christian doctrines of the Trinity, the Incarnation, the Atonement, the necessity of baptism, and the role of the Church in the plan of salvation to be quite incidental. The lodge furthermore exacts a series of oaths from its candidates which cannot be called valid extrajudicial oaths; those who swear such oaths, agreeing to the most horrible self-mutilation in order to protect a few passwords and secret grips, are objectively guilty of either vain or rash swearing. Third, the Masonic order has historically sought to destroy the Catholic Church and to substitute a purely secular society. Posing as nonpartisan in religious affairs the lodge plumps for abolishment of parochial schools, easy divorce laws, cremation, suppression of religious orders especially the Society of Jesus, and a separation of Church and State never envisioned by the framers of the First Amendment. In addition, American Freemasonry discriminates against Negroes, promotes a spirit of religious indifference, lends itself to manifold injustices through preferential treatment of Masons by Masons, and expunges the name of Christ from lodge prayers and from Bible passages used in the ritual.

Pope Clement directed his bull *In Eminenti* (April 28, 1738) against Francis, Grand Duke of Tuscany, who had sponsored Masonic lodges within his domain. The bull read in part:

> It has become known to us, even in truth by public rumor, that great and extensive progress is being made by, and the strength daily increasing of, some Societies, Meetings, Gatherings, Conventicles or Lodges commonly known as of Liberi Muratori, or Freemasons or some other nomenclature according to difference of language, in which men of any religion and sect whatsoever, content with a certain affectation of natural virtue, are associated mutually in a close and exclusive bond in accordance with laws and statutes framed for themselves; and

are bound as well by a stringent oath sworn upon the Sacred Volume, as by the imposition of heavy penalties to conceal under inviolable silence, what they secretly do in their meetings.

But since it is the nature of wickedness to betray itself, and to cry aloud so as to reveal itself, hence the aforesaid Societies or Conventicles have excited so strong suspicion in the minds of the faithful that to enroll oneself in these Lodges is quite the same, in the judgment of prudent and virtuous men, as to incur the brand of depravity and perverseness, for if they were not acting ill, they would not by any means have such a hatred of the light. And this repute has spread to such a degree that in very many countries the societies just mentioned have been proscribed, and with foresight banished long since as though hostile to the safety of kingdoms.

We, accordingly, turning over in our mind the very serious injuries which are in the highest degree inflicted by such Societies or Conventicles not merely on the tranquillity of the temporal state, but also on the spiritual welfare of souls, and perceiving that they are inconsistent alike with civil and canonical sanctions, being taught by the divine word that it is our duty, by day and night, like a faithful servant, and a prudent ruler of his master's household, to watch that no persons of this kind like thieves break into the house, and like foxes strive to ravage the vineyard, that is to say, thereby pervert the hearts of the simple and privily shoot at the innocent; in order to close the wide road which might be opened thereby for perpetrating iniquity with impunity and for other just and reasonable causes known to ourselves, have determined and decreed that these same Societies, Meetings, Gatherings, Lodges or Conventicles, of Liberi Muratori, or Freemasons, or by whatever other name called, herein acting on the advice of some Venerable Brethren of ours, Cardinals of the Holy Roman Church, and also of our own motion, and from our certain knowledge, and mature deliberation, and in the plenitude of Apostolic Power, should be condemned and prohibited as by this present Constitution we do condemn and prohibit them.

Wherefore we direct the faithful in Christ, all and singly, of whatever status, grade, dignity and preeminence, whether laics or clerics as well secular as regular, even those worthy of specific and individual mention and expression, strictly and in virtue of holy obedience, that no one, under any pretext or farfetched color dare or presume to enter the above mentioned Societies of Liberi Muratori, Freemasons, or otherwise named, or to propagate, foster and receive them whether in their houses or elsewhere, and to conceal them, or be present at them, or to afford them the opportunity or facilities for being convened anywhere, or otherwise to render them advice, help or favor, openly or in secret, directly or indirectly, of themselves or through the agency of others in whatever way; and likewise to exhort, induce, incite or persuade others to be enrolled in, reckoned among, or take part in Societies of this kind, or to aid and foster them in any way whatsoever; but in every particular to abstain utterly as they are in duty bound from the same Societies, Meetings, Assemblies, Gatherings, Lodges, or Conventicles, on pain of excommunication to be incurred by all who in the above ways offend — to be incurred ipso facto without any declaration, and that from this excommunication no one, except on the point of death, can obtain benefit of absolution except through Us, or the Roman Pontiff for the time being.

Communications in 1738 did not encompass the daily newspapers, magazines, radio, TV, and motion pictures of today, and hence the Catholic world did not immediately know of the contents of the bull. According to ancient Church practice a bull was not promulgated in a given diocese until it is posted and means are obtained to enforce it. Where Masonry was not yet a problem or where secular authorities prevailed upon individual bishops the promulgation was delayed for many years. To add to the confusion a bogus bull was circulated which asked the faithful to support the lodges whenever possible!

Consequently we find that some Catholics, particularly in Ireland, continued to join the lodge after the papal pronouncement. Some served as Worshipful Masters and some lodges were composed entirely of Catholic priests and laymen. Even the Irish patriot Daniel O'Connell served as Master of Dublin Lodge No. 189 after his initiation in 1799. In 1837 he testified that he had renounced the lodge some years before. Lord Petre, a prominent Roman Catholic, became Grand Master of the English lodge in 1772 and served in this capacity for five years.

Daniel Carroll, brother of the first American bishop, was active in Masonry and apparently Bishop Carroll did not consider the papal ban applicable to this country until sometime after 1800. For example, the bishop discussed the various censures of the Holy See on the lodge question in a letter to a layman in 1794. He added, "I do not pretend that these decrees are received generally by the Church, or have full authority in this diocese." A convent of nuns in Nantes sent a Masonic apron to George Washington as a present. Masons laid the cornerstone for St. Mary's church, first Catholic church in Albany and first cathedral of that diocese. Catholics in the Louisiana Territory were likely to be members of the lodge and Father Sedella, pastor of the New Orleans cathedral, was buried in Masonic regalia.

Clement's successor, Pope Benedict XIV, was equally adamant against the spreading secret societies, especially Freemasonry. He asked Maria Theresa, Empress of Austria, to disband the lodge in Vienna. Police almost arrested her husband, Francis, when they raided the lodge room but the Duke escaped through a back door. The captured Masons were detained for a day or two but the lodge soon resumed underground activities. Benedict issued a second bull in 1751 reiterating the penalty of excommunication.

Present-day readers may consider some of the papal charges to be wide of the mark. Masons delight in pointing to distinguished American statesmen and asking if these are the depraved and perverted men whom the popes identify. At the same time the only Catholic Church which Masonic polemicists seem to know at firsthand is the Church of the Spanish Inquisition. Masons should remember that these early bulls against the lodge were written long before the American Revolution. When the popes say "now" in these bulls they mean the mid-1700's and when they spoke of Masonry they meant the European Masonry which they knew. That the charges in these pronouncements blacken the character of the neighborhood druggist or filling station operator who joined the local F. & A. M. lodge to sell more pills or gasoline or just to get away for an evening with the boys would be a just criticism if we ignored the time and circumstances. Today, more than two centuries later, the character of individual Masons is not the point; Catholics are warned against the enticements of the lodge but not because the lodge promotes communism or perversion or subversion or carousing or atheism.

Pius VII (1821), Leo XII (1825), Pius VIII (1829), and Gregory XVI (1832) issued bulls against Freemasonry and the host of secret societies which were infesting the continent and thriving on intrigue, assassination, and subversion. Freethinkers flocked to the lodges as the natural base from which to attack Church and State. Today the same sort of person would naturally gravitate toward the Socialist and Communist parties which promise to overthrow the present social order. Italian Masonry was disrupted by feuds and schisms but the chief leaders of the Italian unification movement were all Masons: Mazzini, Garibaldi, and Cavour.

Pope Pius IX issued six bulls on Freemasonry between 1846 and 1873. His 1865 Allocution pointed out:

> Among the numerous machinations and artifices by which the enemies of the Christian name have tried to attack the Church of God, and sought to shake it and besiege it by efforts superfluous in truth must undoubtedly be reckoned that perverse society of men called Masonic, which at first confined to darkness and obscurity, now comes into light for the common ruin of religion and human society.

Bishop John McGill of Richmond castigated the lodge in a pastoral letter published in 1884:

> (Masonry) professes a great respect for religion, declaring that only men who respect religion can be members, and it amuses its members with a display of the Bible and certain prayers and religious terms, and while it inculcates the belief that the love of man and mere human virtues are all-sufficient and alone necessary, and in this manner it more effectually combats Christianity than can be done by the hosts of immoral and infidel writers who are openly laboring for its destruction. It is mighty in its agency, because it professes to dispose of the goods of the present life. It places its sword at the entrance of all the avenues of trade, business and professional life, and gives the accolade of patronage and success only to those who have learned its catechism and been initiated through the means of its supernatural signs. Its influence seriously affects all who refuse to enroll their names upon its list, upon all the fields of competition, and follows its members with the benefits of aid and protection upon the battlefields, in the prisons, before the tribunals of justice, and at the hustings. It throws the veil of concealment over its chief end and its internal administration by the requirements of a solemn oath of secrecy, and only makes itself known to the public by its festive processions with dazzling banners and regalia, and by its bountiful donations and timely assistance to the widows and orphans of deceased members.

The notorious Leo Taxil case illustrates the credibility of some Catholics on the subject of Masonry. Although the hoax was exposed, some of the fantastic ideas about Masonry linger in Catholic folklore. Likewise, Masonic partisans point to the Taxil case as proof positive that the Church's case against the lodge is built on falsehoods and misunderstandings.

Taxil, a French anticlerical journalist, had written a sensational pot boiler called *Secret Amours of Pius IX* and he now saw another chance to get rich quick and humiliate the Church he despised. He pretended conversion, recanted his atheist writings, and was received into the Church. He published a series of books entitled *Complete Revelations of French Masonry* in which he accused the lodges of demon worship, orgies, spiritualism, Black Masses, etc. Masons were guilty of every crime from ritual murder to blasphemy according to convert Taxil who added that worship of Satan was the object of the higher degrees. He claimed that Charleston, S. C., then headquarters of the Scottish Rite Southern Jurisdiction, was the fountainhead of diabolical Masonry with Pike as the Masonic pope. The high priestess of higher Masonry, a being with supernatural powers who was known as "Diana," rebelled when Pike commanded her to desecrate a host. She too authored books on Masonry which were ghost written by Taxil.

Taxil was acclaimed as an outstanding authority on the inner workings of Masonry and was featured speaker at an anti-Masonic congress at Trent in 1896. The 1000 delegates clamored for an appearance by the mysterious Diana and Taxil promised to produce her in Paris on Easter Monday, 1897. Instead the anti-Masonic mountebank astonished his admirers by announcing that his conversion 12 years earlier was a pretense, Diana a myth, and his revelations pure fiction.

The unbelievable gullibility of some Catholics in the Taxil case may serve as a wholesome lesson in examining Masonry. The Christian case against the lodge will never be served by checking intelligence and common sense at the door. During the course of research on this book the author has heard tales of Masonic doings hardly less incredible than Taxil's famous fabrications. One clergyman solemnly described the death lottery in which all 33rd degree Masons participate. Every year one name is drawn and the winner (loser) must agree to commit suicide in the following year for the greater glory of Freemasonry!

On the other hand, we cannot absolve the Masons for resorting to wild exaggeration and fables in seeking to discredit the papal condemnations. For years they circulated the canard that Popes Benedict XIV and Pius IX had themselves been initiated into the lodge. Such preposterous stories have been retold in the pages of the *New Age* although they have the same sort of historical basis as the legend of Pope Joan. In a solemn allocution on April 20, 1849, Pius IX referred to the rumor about his Masonic initiation and denounced it as "the blackest of all calumnies."

One of the greatest modern popes, Leo XIII, was also one of Masonry's stanchest foes. This has embarrassed those Masons who argue that only political reactionaries among the hierarchy used the lodge as a red herring to divert the attention of the people from needed social reforms. Because of its paramount importance in understanding the position of the Church on Freemasonry we have reproduced the encyclical, *Humanum genus*, in full in the Appendix. In this 1884 encyclical Pope Leo indicates that the human race is divided into two opposing camps, one under God and the other under Satan. "At every period of time each has been in conflict with the other, with a variety and multiplicity of weapons, and of warfare, although not always with equal ardor and assault. At this period, however, the partisans of evil seem to be combining together, and to be struggling with united vehemence, led on or assisted by that strongly organized and widespread association called the Freemasons," declared the pontiff. Of course, the Holy Father did not mean that all Masons are wicked and all Christians, saintly. He is speaking of the spirit of the Church and the spirit of Masonic naturalism as unalterably opposed to one another. Pike replied to the pope's denunciation by delivering a Praelocution in October, 1884. This consisted mainly in a recital of alleged horrors of the Inquisition and misdeeds of the Church of Rome. Said the head of the Southern Jurisdiction of the Scottish Rite, "If, in other countries, Freemasonry has lost sight of the Ancient Landmarks, even tolerating communism and atheism, it is better to endure ten years of these evils than it would be to live a week under the devilish tyranny of the Inquisition and of the black soldiery of Loyola. Atheism is a dreary unbelief, but it at least does not persecute, torture, or roast men who believe there is a God." Tragically, history and international Communism have proved General Pike to be wrong.

The General went out of his way to deny any basic distinction between American and Latin and Continental Masonry:

> It is not when the powers of the Papacy are concentrated to crush the Freemasonry of the Latin Kingdoms and Republics of the world, that the Masons of the Ancient and Accepted Scottish Rite in the United States will, from any motive whatever, proclaim that they have no sympathy with the Masons of the Continent of Europe, or with those of Mexico or of the South American Republics. If these fall into errors of practice or indulge in extravagances of dogma, we will dissent and remonstrate; but we will not forget that the Freemasonry of our Rite and of the French Rite has always been the Apostle of Civil and Religious Liberty, and that the blood of Spanish and other Latin Freemasons has again and again glorified and sanctified the implements of torture, the scaffold and the stake, of the Papacy and the Inquisition.

In a later reply to the encyclical Pike boasts:

> It is the crowning glory of Freemasonry that, requiring only that a Candidate shall believe and put his trust in a living and personal God, a beneficent and protecting Providence, to whom it is not folly to pray; and shall believe in the continued existence of the Soul of man after the death of the body, it receives into its Lodges the Christian of every sect, the Hebrew, the Moslem and the Parsee, and unites them in the holy bonds of brotherhood.

Pope Leo's final word on Freemasonry was delivered in 1902. The official position of the Church regarding membership in the lodge was stated in the Code of Canon Law issued by Benedict XV in 1917. Since then the Holy See has been preoccupied with the immense problems of two world wars, the rise of nationalism, Fascism, and Nazism, the tremendous advance of atheistic Communism which has engulfed 800 million people, the possibilities of H-bomb annihilation. The position of the Church on Freemasonry could not be made clearer and the recent pontiffs have not felt the need to restate what their predecessors have repeatedly declared.

The late Pope Pius XII, however, may have had Masonry in mind in his 1955 May Day address when he warned, "Laws and institutions are of little worth if the ordinary man sees in his daily life that everything depends on influential connections which he, unlike others, does not possess; or if he suspects that behind the façade of what is called the State there lies concealed the manipulations of powerful organized groups."

For more than 200 years the Catholic Church has called attention to the anti-Christian basis of modern Masonry. What originated as Catholic guilds engaged in erecting the magnificent cathedrals of the Middle Ages has become one of the implacable enemies of the Church. The points on which the lodge stands condemned are not the peculiarities of the French Grand Orient or other "schismatic" Masonic bodies. The recent popes, particularly Leo XIII, were well aware that the bulk of the world's Masons were English and American. Their lodges have been condemned for their religious naturalism not their atheism, for their immoral oaths, for their historic if technically unofficial anticlericalism. As we shall see, millions of Protestant and Eastern Orthodox Christians belong to denominations which join in warning against affiliation with the Masonic sect.

CHAPTER IX

ALLIED MASONIC ORGANIZATIONS

Shrine, DeMolay, Eastern Star Limited to
Masons and Relatives

The 805,000 red fezzed Shriners revel in Islamic shenanigans, sponsor boisterous national conventions, raise millions of dollars through circuses and the East-West football game to support their 17 hospitals for crippled children, and top the list of some 60 allied Masonic organizations in this country.

This extensive network of Masonic-related associations includes some for Masons, their wives, sons, daughters, and relatives; for Masons in college and in the armed forces; for Masons interested in the history of the Craft, social activities, ancient rites, charities, writing, and Masonic philosophy.

None of these three-score associations constitutes an official Masonic society since pure Masonry is confined to the three Blue Lodge degrees (and possibly the Royal Arch). But they are all limited in membership to Masons and their relatives and all promote the interests of the lodge.

Membership in the Ancient Arabic Order Nobles of the Mystic Shrine is open only to Masons who are Knights Templar or 32nd degree Masons in the Scottish rite. Blue Lodge Masons who make up the bulk of the nation's 4,100,000 Masons may caper and cavort in local Grottos or Forests of the Tall Cedars of Lebanon. Unless they choose to climb the York or Scottish rite ladders of "higher" degrees they remain ineligible for the Mystic Shrine.

The claim that the Shrine is the American branch of an honorable centuries old Arabian vigilante society forms part of the ritual but like many Masonic traditions must be rejected as pure fabrication. As this discredited story goes, the American comedian William J. (Billy) Florence joined the Shrine in Cairo through the kind offices of the reigning Sultan. He and Dr. Walter M. Fleming transplanted the Shrine to American shores and founded the first temple in New York City in 1871. Unfortunately no trace of any such organization has been found in Moslem lands nor has any documentary evidence been produced to indicate a history prior to 1871. The few Shriners who bother with Shrine history discount the Arabian origin of the Ancient Arabic Order.

The original Mecca temple all but petered out in a few years until it was revived by Florence in 1875. In the meantime the comedian incorporated elements of mysterious Oriental rites he had witnessed in Marseilles — or so he said. Hannah credits Florence and Dr. Fleming, both 33rd degree Masons, with authorship of the "adolescent and occasionally Rabelaisian nadir of drivelling tom-foolery and burlesque blasphemies which serves as its ritual." Shrinedom is clothed in the very Moslem symbols which struck terror in the hearts of the Christian communities of the Near East, Africa, and Southern Europe. The candidate swears to protect the Koran and the Mohammedan faith. He wears the crescent and scimitar which for centuries has represented the fanatic faith which snuffed out the Church of Christ in North Africa. The Shriner does not die but "answers the call of the Black Camel."

Of course, we readily admit that no Shriner seriously commits himself to the Islamic faith or considers the oaths he has freely given on the Bible and the Koran as such a profession of faith. Just as the Mason may have played at being a Christian in the Knights Templar rites so now he plays at being a Moslem. Perhaps in a few years another comedian and another physician will concoct a Hindu or Buddhist ritual for the edification of Christian gentlemen.

As many as 300 or 400 candidates "cross the burning sands" in the initiation ceremony. They must have met Masonic membership requirements, paid an initiation fee ranging from $100, and gathered at one of the 160 Temples.

After preliminary interrogations and platitudes, the High Priest welcomes the prospective Nobles: "By the existence of Allah and the creed of Mohammed, by the legendary sanctity of our Tabernacle at Mecca, we greet you, and in commemoration of the Arab's faith in purity and innocence, we accept your answers as sincere, and you will now be permitted to proceed in the rites and ceremonies of the Mystic Shrine." At the black Altar of Obligation which supports a Bible and a copy of the Koran the candidates take the following obligation:

"——, of my voluntary desire, uninfluenced and of free accord, do hereby assume, without reserve, the Obligation of the Nobility of the Mystic Shrine, as did the elect of the Temple of Mecca, the Moslem and the Mohammedan. I do hereby, upon this Bible, and on the mysterious legend of the Koran, and its dedication to the Mohammedan faith, promise and swear and vow on the faith and honor of an upright man, come weal or woe, adversity or success, that I will never reveal any secret part or portion whatsoever of the ceremonies I have already received, that are about to be communicated to me and that I may hereafter be instructed in, to any person in the world, except it be to a well-known member of the Order of Nobles of the Mystic Shrine, and I, knowing to an absolute certainty that he or they may be truly and lawfully such, and of good standing with such Nobility. That I will not be present, aid or countenance the conferring of the Order of the Mystic Shrine upon any person who is not a Masonic Knight Templar or a thirty-second degree A. and A. Scottish Rite Mason in good standing.

"I further promise and vow that I will not willfully write, cut, speak or portray any detail that might be construed into even a clue to the same, except for official Temple work.

"Furthermore, I do here register a sacred vow, promising, should I live to become a member, I will impartially cast a black ballot without fear or favor against friend or foe applying for membership in the Nobility of the Mystic Shrine, whom I believe to be disgraced, dishonored, a thief, a perjurer, a murderer, a lunatic, an idiot or a criminal. And should I undismayed pass safely through the Moslem test and be found worthy of the confidence of my fellows albeit I do not actively espouse the cause, still I do promise to be silent, even if neutral, and not oppose the purposes of the order.

"I further promise and vow that I will obey the laws and submit to the decrees of the Parent Temple, the Imperial Grand Council of the United States of America, and that I will not acknowledge, recognize nor be present in any other body of Nobles of the Mystic Shrine, claiming to be Superior in authority, nor be present in any clandestine Temple not holding constitutional authority from the Imperial Grand Council of the Mystic Shrine.

"I furthermore promise and vow that to the full measure of my ability I will never swerve from justice nor duty. That I will respect virtue; protect the innocent; assist the distressed; promote the inculcation of honor and integrity and dispense reasonable charity. That I will protect and defend the unsullied honor of any Noble of the Mystic Shrine, when absent, if assailed; and now upon this sacred book, by the sincerity of a Moslem's oath I here register this irrevocable vow, subscribing myself bound thereto as well as binding myself by the obligation of the prerequisite to this membership, that of a Knight Templar or that of a thirty-second degree A. and A. Scottish Rite Mason. In willful violation wherof may I incur the fearful penalty of having my eyeballs pierced to the center with a three-edged blade, my feet flayed and I be forced to walk the hot sands upon the sterile shores of the Red Sea until the flaming sun shall strike me with livid plague, and may Allah, the god of Arab Moslem and Mohammedan, the god of our fathers, support me to the entire fulfillment of the same, Amen. Amen. Amen."

At the conclusion of this blasphemous oath the candidates are asked to kiss the Christian Bible, not the Koran, "as a token of your sincerity."

With an unwieldy number of prospective Nobles, lots are drawn and only a few are subjected to the following endurance tests and pranks. The rest may remove their blindfolds and enjoy the spectacle of their brothers' discomfort.

Among the pranks engineered during the remainder of the initiation are the Bung hole test in which two blindfolded candidates enter opposite ends of a large metal cylinder and bump heads in the middle. As the two participants lie down for a minute's rest after this ordeal one of the Nobles yelps like a small dog while another squirts a few drops of warm water in the candidate's face. A fellow Noble indignantly demands, "Take that dog out of here. He has just p—— in the face of Mr. ——!" Other candidates are instructed to stoop low to receive the Grand Salaam which consists of a blow by two pieces of board which are set to explode small torpedoes on contact.

Now another candidate for the Nobility is stripped to shirt, drawers, and slippers and led around the room several times. Finally the Conductor says, "This is the place where our brethren stop to sprinkle the Devil's Pass with urine. You will contribute a few drops of urine to commemorate the time and place where all who pass here renounce the wiles and evils of the world to worship at the Shrine of Islam. Only a few drops will do." As the candidate begins to comply, his blindfold is jerked off and he beholds a group of women staring at him (disguised Nobles). He retreats in confusion. Later the Nobles stage a mock hanging and beheading and pretend to drink the blood from the severed head. The initiation closes with a banquet.

English Masonry would never countenance the poor taste of the Shrine ritual nor the general silliness of Shrine exhibitions. This puerile ritual would embarrass many college fraternity pledge masters and only Christians with a singular lack of historical sense and fitness would pattern a society after Christendom's ancient persecutors. Perhaps a hundred years from now a similar gathering of professed Christians will sport red hammer and sickles in their lapels and address each other as Comrades in Main Street Kremlins.

The one real contribution of the Shriners is their chain of hospitals for crippled children, a magnificent charity for which they deserve everyone's gratitude. For 50 years after its founding the

Mystic Shrine was purely and simply the playground for the Masonic elite. In 1920 the Imperial Potentate called upon the Nobles to devote some of their energies to a worthier goal. He recommended that they tax themselves $2 per capita annually to establish a series of hospitals for crippled children unable to pay for medical treatment.

Since then more than 250,000 children under 14 have been admitted to Shriners' orthopedic hospitals without regard to race, creed, or color. Only those are admitted whose parents are unable to pay for hospitalization or out-patient treatment. Those who can pay are refused admittance. Everything — medical care, clothing, laundry, food, dental care, braces, crutches, and other appliances — is given without cost. It seems, however, that the Shriners' published boast that this constitutes the "world's greatest philanthropy" is rather extravagant in view of the 927 hospitals, 328 children's homes, 299 homes for the aged and more than 10,000 schools conducted by the Catholic Church in this country alone.

Shriners now contribute at least $5 a year each to support these institutions of which two are in Canada and one each in Hawaii and Mexico. Besides this annual assessment the Shriners also sponsor indoor circuses and the traditional East-West football game which netted more than $250,000 to the San Francisco hospital in one recent year. Bequests also help furnish the $6,500,000 needed to maintain the 17 hospitals each year.

Initiation fees, dues, and assessments are relatively expensive and most Masons never advance in the York or Scottish rites, much less the Shrine. About three out of four eligible Knights Templar and 32nd degree Masons are Shriners. A select group within the Shrine, the Royal Order of Jesters, enrolls about 15,000 members by invitation.

Of the 160 Temples, 149 are in continental United States. Some Temples such as Syria Temple in Pittsburgh with more than 26,000 members have grown so large that the Nobles are likely to know only a small percentage of the Nobility. Temples sponsor bands, glee clubs, and drill teams, own camels, operate country clubs and athletic clubs. Local officers include the Most Illustrious Grand Potentate, Very

Illustrious or Deputy Grand Potentate, the Illustrious Grand Chief Rabban, and the Illustrious Grand High Priest and Prophet. Wives of Shriners have organized the Daughters of the Nile and others have joined the smaller Ladies Oriental Shrine of North America.

Comedian Harold Lloyd followed in Florence's footsteps by serving as Imperial Potentate for a term. Only a wealthy Noble can aspire to this top position since he is expected to visit most or all of the Temples in the country, entertain lavishly, and suspend his regular activities for the year. Three presidents have worn the red fez of the Mystic Shrine: Warren Harding, Franklin D. Roosevelt, and Harry S. Truman.

Approximately 100,000 Nobles attended the 1958 convention in Chicago and spent an estimated $25,000,000 during their stay in that city. The mammoth Shrine parade included 18,000 people and 1,500 horses, camels, and donkeys.

Master Masons make whoopee in the fun organizations of the Blue Lodges: the Grotto and the Forests of the Tall Cedars of Lebanon. The former, formally known as the Mystic Order of Veiled Prophets of the Enchanted Realm, was founded by a postmaster general of the United States, Thomas L. James. He emphasized that "although in many cases the government (of the Grotto) may be guided by Masonic usage as the most perfect system extant, it is to be strictly understood that in itself this is not a Masonic order and the degree is in no sense a Masonic degree." Several lodges in one city or area may support a local Grotto which in turn sponsors dances, dinners, clam bakes, outings, sports activities, etc. The 103,000 Veiled Prophets sport fezzes, contribute to muscular distrophy research, and generally pay less for their whoopla than do the Shriners. The Tall Cedars have only half as many members and maintain Forests in only 10 states. They have taken an interest in cerebral palsy clinics.

Although adoptive or "petticoat" Masonry has been popular in France since 1744, English and American Masons have been reluctant to establish ladies auxiliaries to the lodges. The Order of the Eastern Star confers no Masonic secrets on the ladies but only

Master Masons and their female relatives may join the Order. Today the OES has grown to 3,000,000 members, men and women.

Robert Morris composed the Eastern Star ritual in 1850 but it remained for Robert Macoy, a New York publisher of Masonic literature, to "sell" the auxiliary. By 1884 more than 50,000 women had joined and Negroes who had obtained pirated copies of the ritual launched a parallel order. Eastern Star meetings are usually held in the local Masonic Temples and each OES chapter must include a Master Mason as patron. Originally an advanced OES degree, the White Shrine of Jerusalem is limited to Christians and counts 180,000 members, about half of whom are men. Another former adjunct of the Eastern Star, the Order of Amaranth, numbers 84,000. Incidentally the Grand Lodge of Scotland has recently followed the lead of the English Grand Lodge in forbidding Masons to serve as patrons of the Eastern Star. With such Masonic disapproval the OES barely exists in England and will probably be severely handicapped by the new attitude of the lodge in Scotland.

A popular boys' society, the Order of DeMolay, was founded in Kansas City in 1919 and has remained closely tied to the Scottish rite. DeMolay, last head of the suppressed Knights Templar, was executed in 1314. The Order serves as a novitiate for Masonry and admits male relatives of Master Masons who are between the ages of 14 and 21. About two out of three DeMolays eventually enter the Craft. A competing youth organization, the Order of Builders, is sponsored by the Blue Lodges.

Two societies for teen age girls, both of fairly recent origin, are sponsored by Masons. Job's Daughters was organized in 1921 for Christian girls between 13 and 20 who are related to Masons. They become honorary members on their 20th birthday. The order enrolls about 85,000 girls. The 142,000 Rainbow Girls may continue membership until they reach 21. The latter was founded in 1922 in Oklahoma by the Rev. W. Mack Sexson, 33°.

Following the precedent of English Masonry which forbids initiation of anyone in military lodges below the rank of noncommissioned officer, membership in the National Sojourners is limited to active and retired officers in the armed forces of the United States. Some 350 chapters are found in every major military and naval post in the world. About 14,000 Masonic officers belong to the National Sojourners but enlisted men who happen to be Masons may get together in the informal Square and Compass clubs.

Once restricted to Master Masons, Acacia fraternity now admits Protestant college students who are Masons, sons or brothers of Masons, or who are recommended by two Masons. The fraternity operates chapters on 44 campuses with 17,000 actives. It began at the University of Michigan in 1904.

A sampling of the many other allied Masonic organizations might include: Low Twelve Clubs which maintain funds for death benefits, the Order of Desoms for deaf Masons or deaf men with Masonic relatives, the Order of the Golden Key which aims to establish a Masonic Center of Learning, the Philalethes which serves as a clearinghouse for the exchange of Masonic philosophy, the *Societas Rosicruciana in Civitatibus Foederatis* which studies Masonic history and legends, the Society of Blue Friars which honors Masonic authors, and the Sword of Bunker Hill which promotes patriotism among Masons. Founder Frank Land of the Order of DeMolay unveiled a new Masonic order in 1957, the Ancient and Honorable Guild of the Leather Apron. The Guild hopes to bolster sagging lodge attendance which seldom exceeds 15 per cent of membership.

Considering this panorama of organizations we can easily imagine that a young man could enter the Order of DeMolay at 14, pledge Acacia fraternity at college, enter the Blue Lodge, serve his military obligation as a lieutenant or ensign and affiliate with the National Sojourners, begin his climb in the Masonic hierarchy through either or both the Scottish and York rites, don the fez of the Mystic Shrine, join his wife in the Order of the Eastern Star, and encourage his children to enter Job's Daughters, the Rainbow Girls, DeMolay, or the Order of Builders, etc.

Just as Negroes are refused admittance to white Blue Lodges and to the original Scottish and York rites, so they may not presume to apply for entry into any of these allied organizations. As a result

Negro Masons have set up their own Shrine, Order of the Eastern Star, etc. The Negro counterpart of the Shrine is known as the Ancient Egyptian Arabic Order of the Nobles of the Mystic Shrine for North and South America.

Theoretically Catholics who are converts or who are products of a mixed marriage could qualify for many of these allied organizations through their Masonic relatives. Needless to say the Church forbids such affiliation just as she must forbid initiation into the Masonic order itself. Whatever their special objectives they all seek to further the ideals of the lodge.

We have seen that Jewish Masons are barred from the York rite but the black ball system can also be employed in other branches of Masonry. For example, Ohio Scottish rite officials routinely blackball any applicant for the 32nd degree who lists a rabbi as his religious reference. This discrimination is common knowledge among Jewish Masons in that state.

CHAPTER X

LATIN AND EUROPEAN MASONRY

Grand Orients Foster Anticlericalism and Atheism

Most non-American Masons are English or citizens of British Commonwealth nations; the number of continental and Latin Masons giving allegiance to the various Grand Orients is relatively small. Nevertheless these Grand Orients rally the anticlerical minorities in their respective nations and historically have stood for bitter hostility to the Christian religion (the Rosicrucians used the term "Orient" to represent Mohammed and "Occident" for the Pope).

Since these Grand Orients no longer require profession of belief in the Supreme Architect or immortality nor use the Bible in administering their Masonic obligations, they are branded Masonic heretics by American and English Masons. They are accused of rejecting traditional landmarks of the Craft.

Masonic claims and anti-Masonic indictments to the contrary, the Masonic order does not form one worldwide fraternity. Anglo-Saxon Masons refuse to recognize the legitimacy of most Grand Orients and disassociate themselves from the open political action and anti-Catholicism of these Masons. The picture of world Masonry resembles the divided state of Christendom rather than the unity of Catholicism. Masonry embraces "orthodox" Anglo-Saxon Masons, heretical Masons in Grand Orients which have discarded essential landmarks, Negro Masons in so-called clandestine lodges, rival

Grand Lodges in several South American nations, and tiny lodges of co-Masonry for the ladies. Individual Masons may express sympathy for irregular bodies but officially their Grand Lodges withhold fraternal relations and visiting privileges from these atheistic Grand Lodges, Negro lodges, and schismatic lodges of various types.

Regular Masons are organized in some 100 independent jurisdictions of which 49 are American and nine Canadian. Most lodges outside the United States are grouped in national Grand Lodges; American lodges are organized in state Grand Lodges and no serious proposals for a central Grand Lodge of the United States have been put forth since the time of Washington. Grand Orients usually claim jurisdiction over both Blue Lodge and "higher degrees."

We have postponed discussion of non-American Masonry for several reasons. First, we wanted to demonstrate that the Christian case against the lodge was not predicated on a condemnation of the openly atheistic Grand Orients but on the naturalism and oaths of Anglo-Saxon Masonry. Second, we believe that American Catholic readers are less interested in the machinations of foreign Masons than in the status of the Craft in this country. Third, American Masonry constitutes by far the largest body of Masons in the world. The Masonic researcher Harold V. B. Voorhis estimated only 33,000 Masons in continental Europe in 1950 compared to nearly 4,000,000 in the United States. Luther A. Smith, Sovereign Grand Commander of the Southern Scottish Rite, estimates there are not more than 60,000 Masons in continental Europe. In his article "Masonry in Europe" he adds: "It is my impression, therefore, that under present social, religious, and political conditions, Freemasonry in Europe has very limited chance for expansion and progress."[1]

English Masonry has cultivated good relations with the crown, the aristocracy, and the Established Church and has scrupulously observed the Masonic landmark against political and religious debate within the lodge. Of course, the queen may not enter into the mysteries of the lodge but her father, George VI, was an active Mason and her husband, the Duke of Edinburgh, was initiated in 1952. The Constitution of the United Grand Lodge stipulates

---

[1] *New Age,* January, 1958, p. 46.

that the Grand Master must be of the nobility. By this triple alliance of crown, church, and lodge the English were able to harness the revolutionary energy of the Masonic lodges which was typically directed against the Church and State on the continent. The present archbishop of Canterbury, Dr. Goeffrey Fisher, is a member of the lodge, the second archbishop of Canterbury in the history of the Church of England to wear the apron. Hannah lists 17 Anglican bishops who have received the higher degrees of the Ancient and Accepted Rite or the Knights Templar.

Such American innovations as the Shrine, DeMolay, and Job's Daughters are unknown in English Masonry which has been most careful to maintain its dignity and decorum. The blatant anti-Catholicism of the Scottish rite's Southern Jurisdiction, the silly antics of the Shriners, and the gruesome skull libations of the American Knights Templar would not be tolerated by English Masons.

In 1874 Grand Master the Marquess of Ripon shocked English Freemasonry by resigning from the supreme post of the Craft to enter the Catholic Church. He had served as Grand Master for four years. His successor was the playboy Prince of Wales who resigned his Grand Mastership in 1901 to become Edward VII. Edward's brother, the Duke of Connaught, served as Grand Master for 38 years.

Some 550,000 Masons are enrolled in the 6750 English lodges while another 400,000 belong to the less expensive but more popular Scottish lodges. Masonic membership in Ireland is confined to the Protestant minority and totals fewer than 47,000. But at the end of the eighteenth century the Craft counted more lodges in Ireland than in England; the eventual promulgation of the papal bulls against Masonry depleted the Irish lodges. Traces of the Christian heritage of the Craft may still be found in Irish workings and the name of Christ may be used in lodge prayers when its use will not offend anyone present. Irish Catholic critics of the lodge have seen Masonry as an ally of the hated British and Protestant landlords and have too often been inclined to exaggerate the role of Masonry in world affairs.

Even small English towns of 4000 or 5000 support two or three Masonic lodges of varying social prestige. The oldest or "snob" lodge will enroll the best people of the community. Initiation fees range from five to 25 pounds. The largest cities such as London, Birmingham, and Liverpool include a number of "class" lodges which are open to members of certain professions. For example, the Mendelsohn Lodge in London enrolls only musicians. Most exclusive of these lodges is the Guildhall Lodge for Aldermen only; its initiation fee is reported to be 100 pounds.

From England the Craft spread to France with the chartering of the lodge *Amitie et Fraternite* at Dunkerque in 1721. Not content with the three degrees of the Blue Lodge, the French Masonic enthusiasts invented scores of higher degrees most of which have become museum pieces. Occultism infiltrated French Masonry to a greater degree than the parent body and the Grand Orient drifted from deism to atheism.

Both opponents and partisans of Freemasonry have claimed that the lodges played a larger share in the French Revolution than history indicates. Most French Masons were royalists who would not be expected to encourage the extreme republicanism of the Revolution. In 1793 the Grand Master of the Grand Orient, Philippe-Egalite, resigned his position and the lodges deteriorated for several years. The famous Catholic lay leader, Count de Maistre, was proud to be an Ultramontane and a Freemason.

The *New Age* for June, 1957, carried a eulogistic article by a 33rd degree Mason about another Mason, Voltaire. In a letter to Damilaville, Brother Voltaire wrote:

> The Christian religion is an infamous religion, an abominable hydra which must be destroyed by a hundred invisible hands. It is necessary that the philosophers should course through the streets to destroy it as missionaries course over earth and sea to propagate it. They ought to dare all things, risk all things, even to be burned, in order to destroy it. Let us crush the wretch! Crush the wretch!

Napoleon, whose Masonic status is uncertain, sought to control the lodges as well as the Church. He made his brother Joseph Grand Master of the Grand Orient in 1805. Gradually the aristocrats took less interest in the lodge and their places were taken by merchants, bureaucrats, journalists, and lawyers. Napoleon III nominated Marshall Magnan as Grand Master even though his nominee was not a Mason and had to hustle through all 33 degrees in a single day.

When in 1877 the Grand Orient removed from its Constitutions the requirement of belief in the Supreme Architect and discontinued the use of the V.S.L. in administering the oath, the Grand Lodges of the world ostracized the French lodges as "heretical." The Grand Orient's action was designed to accommodate a number of Positivists who wished to enter the fraternity without subscribing to a belief in a Supreme Being. A French Protestant pastor was brought forward to explain to Masons in other countries that this action by the Grand Orient did not actually mean an endorsement of atheism.

From the fall of the MacMahon government in 1877 until World War II Masons held the reins of the French government. Religious orders were disbanded and expelled and Church schools were forced to close. Typical of the sentiments of the French lodge were those of Senator Delpech given at a Masonic banquet in 1902:

> The triumph of the Galilean has lasted twenty centuries; he is dying in his turn. The mysterious voice which once on the mountains of Epirus announced the death of Pan, today announces the death of the deceiver God who had promised an era of justice and peace to those who should believe in him. The illusion has lasted very long; the lying God in his turn disappears; he goes to rejoin in the dust of ages the other divinities of India, Egypt, Greece, and Rome, who saw so many deluded creatures throw themselves at the foot of their altars. Freemasons, we are pleased to state that we are not unconcerned with this ruin of false prophets. The Roman Church, founded on the Galilean myth, began to decline rapidly on the day when the Masonic association was constituted. From the political point of view Freemasons have often varied. But in all times Freemasonry has stood firm on this principle: war on all superstitions, war on all fanaticism.

During this same period of Masonic ascendancy in France the notorious *affaire des fiches* was exposed. The Grand Orient kept index cards on each army officer indicating if the officer attended Mass, allowed other members of his family to practice their religion, sent his children to religious instruction, encouraged religion among his troops, etc. These cards were forwarded to the War Department and those who were guilty of such Christian practices were ineligible for promotion and assigned to the least desirable posts. Over 18,000 officers were thus blacklisted by the Grand Orient between 1901 and 1904 before photographic evidence was produced to expose the conspiracy. The revelation demoralized the French army and revealed the power of the Masonic minority in that nation.

A rival Masonic body, the Grand Loge Nationale, was established in Paris in 1914 by dissidents who wished to restore the use of the Bible and the invocation to the Grand Architect. This new Grand Lodge won recognition from the English lodge and has since had modest success. Marshall Petain suppressed both Masonic bodies during World War II. Masonry no longer attracts the militant anticlerical who now finds other outlets for expressing his hatred of Christianity. The domination of French political life by Masons seems to be over.

In recent years German Masons must have felt that they were living through times "when a fella needs a friend." The German lodges were barely tolerated by orthodox Lutherans, condemned by Catholics, disbanded by the Nazis, scorned by the Communists and Socialists, and usually closed to Jews. The "Humanitarian" lodges in Hamburg and Frankfort would admit a few Jews but the "Christian" lodges of Prussia and Berlin were traditionally anti-Semitic.

Hamburg was the site of the first German lodge in 1737 and we have seen that Frederick the Great dabbled in the Craft at one stage in his career. Goethe, Mozart, Haydn, and Fichte were among the Masonic initiates in the eighteenth century and most of the Prussian officers and many members of the Hohenzollern dynasty joined in the nineteenth century. As many as eight independent Grand Lodges were functioning in Germany at one time. Hitler outlawed the lodge, confiscated its temples and paraphernalia, and practically obliterated all traces of Masonry in the Third Reich. Today about 14,000 German Masons are grouped in 250 West German lodges. American military officers have been instrumental in the postwar Masonic revival in Germany.

The patronage of royalty has given Scandinavian Masonry a

prestige which it has not enjoyed elsewhere except in England. The sovereigns are hereditary Grand Masters of these lodges which enroll a much more select membership than in either England or America. For example, there are only about 10,000 Masons in Norway, 23,000 in Sweden, and 213 in Finland (which included the late Sibelius). Scandinavian Masonry is barely recognizable, combining the York and Scottish rite with Christian and Swedenborgian elements.

The Belgian lodge has become so deeply involved in politics that it has been disowned by most other branches of the Craft. The first Belgian lodge was opened in 1770 and gained independence from French control in 1814. Brussels University, the only university in Europe not founded by the Church or State, was established by Freemasons in 1834 as a rival to the Catholic University of Louvain. Belgian Freemasons have been leaders in the campaign against Catholic schools and wield considerable power in the government. Naturally the Catholic royal family does not patronize the lodge.

The Dutch Grand Orient was formed in 1758 and maintains cordial relations with Grand Lodges in England and America. There are only 5000 Blue Lodge Masons in the Netherlands and 500 of these have also joined the Scottish rite. No one petitions to join the Scottish rite in Holland; Blue Lodge members are observed, tested, and eventually invited to join.

Austrian Freemasonry was promoted by Francis I but checked by the opposition of the Church and the Empress Maria Theresa. An edict in 1801 forbade any civil servant from belonging to or attending a secret society. The Nazis' suppression wiped out the remnants of Freemasonry in this country although a modest revival has been reported.

Joseph Bonaparte encouraged the spread of the lodge in Spain and the aggressively political and anticlerical Spanish lodges contributed to Spanish unrest for decades. Generalissimo Franco has banned Masonic activity altogether and if any Spanish Masons remain they operate underground. English Masons were unable to recognize the Spanish Grand Orient because of various irregularities. A character in Gironella's *The Cypresses Believe in God* expressed one Spanish viewpoint:

> Is the antiquity they [the Masons] ascribe to themselves true? What a question! They claim it so as not to float in a void. . . . As a matter of fact, the Masons were formerly nothing but theosophists, alchemists, *illumines* . . . carrying on individual activities or working in small groups. Later they organized into separate corporations to protest against the social disciplines imposed by the Church. But there were no disciplined lodges, with a constitution they obeyed, until 1717. The thing began in England. Since then they have constituted themselves a church, with a hierarchy, liturgy, dogmas, even rewards and punishments. . . .
>
> Now, I'm going to show you that I am not a fanatic who sees sea lions in the mountains. With regard to religion, the attitude of the Masons varies. The Anglo-Saxons have always maintained a certain spiritual tone, with their philanthropic works, their mutual aid, and the restraint they display. Possibly they are the worst of all, for they have always proceeded without scruples and, with the support of the Empire, have tried to make themselves the masters of the world. But even though their attacks on the Roman Church have been ferocious, at least they did not reject the idea of God, even though it was a God in their own image, an English God, a Mason or a cricket-player. . . . The Grand Orient of France officially declared itself atheist, anti-church, secular in its constitutions. It swore to exterminate the clergy, and declared war on every mystic or simply spiritual idea. Man, with a capital was free, the Absolute did not exist because it ran counter to the achievements of evolution. . . . The men governing Spain are all linked to French Freemasonry. Prieto, Martinez Barrios and the rest belong to the Grand Orient, and are thirty-third degree Masons. . . .
>
> I'm not denying that there have been Masons who were idealists, who acted in good faith. But most of them were moved by a desire for temporal power, resentment against Almighty God, and hatred of the triumph of the Church. They could not accept *Thou art Peter, and upon this rock I will build my Church.* That's why their work carries the stigma of the Devil. Every step they took has been a misfortune for humanity, sometimes without their even being aware of it.[2]

In neighboring Portugal Masonic politicians gained control of the nation in 1910 and set up a republic with the following Constitutional provisions:

---

[2] Jose Maria Gironella, *The Cypresses Believe in God* (New York: Alfred A. Knopf, 1955), pp. 386–387.

Ministers of religion shall have no part in the parochial lay corporations or associations in charge of temporal affairs. A minister of religion who criticizes or attacks any of the acts of a public authority or the form of government or the laws of the Republic or any of the provisions of the present law will be punishable by law. Church property shall belong to the State, but shall be loaned to the Church. The wearing of the clerical habit outside of the churches and ceremonies is prohibited. It is also prohibited to publish in any way by word or deed, any bulls, decrees, or communications from the Roman Curia, or prelates, or others, without explicit permission from the civil authorities. The State will have charge of naming and approving the professors in ecclesiastical seminaries for the training of priests and will determine the text-books and courses of study therein. No Jesuits or other monastic orders or religious congregations shall be admitted into Portuguese territory. All Jesuits, whether aliens, naturalized citizens, or natives, are expelled, and all their real or personal property is confiscated. As for the members of other religious orders, if they are aliens or naturalized citizens, they are likewise to be expelled, and if they are natives, they must return to secular life, or at least may not live in community, and shall not be allowed to exercise the teaching profession or intervene in any way in education.

The present head of the Portuguese state, Salazar, has denied the Masonic order legal status and the land visited by Our Lady of Fatima has been delivered from the Grand Orient's blight.

Carried to Italy in 1733 the Masonic order was first known there as the "Company of the Trowel." With the rise of the revolutionary Carbonari and Young Italy movements between 1814 and 1860 the lodges were eclipsed. Garibaldi formed a Grand Orient in Palermo in 1860 and at Mazzini's funeral in 1872 Masonic banners were seen on the streets of Rome. Although Mussolini included a number of Masons in his first government, he soon turned on the lodge and extinguished Freemasonry in Fascist Italy. The dictator ordered all Masonic emblems removed from Garibaldi monuments and replaced with fasces and axes. Today the lodges are once again free to reorganize although the predominately Catholic population knows the ecclesiastical penalty for affiliation. The Grand Lodge of Italy now has 120 chartered lodges and 3700 members with 2000 in the Scottish rite. This is only one of several competing Grand Lodges in that country.

Strong opposition by the Church of Greece (Orthodox) handicapped the growth of the Craft in that country. The 50 or so lodges were destroyed during World War II but efforts at revival have been made with American assistance. King George, a member of the Church of Greece, defied the pronouncements of the bishops by becoming a Mason during his exile in England. Recently the Grand Lodge of Greece circulated a letter to all other Grand Lodges urging them to apply pressure on their respective governments to allow Cyprus to return to Greece. The English Masons were outraged and sent a joint reply with the Grand Lodges of Scotland and Ireland protesting this violation of the "no politics" rule.

Turkey was to secret societies what Los Angeles has been to religious cults before the rise of Kemal Ataturk. Ataturk used his Masonic membership to advantage in his seizure of power and then denounced the lodge and closed its Turkish temples.

Abortive attempts have been made to establish the Craft in Rumania and Yugoslavia but even before the war these countries proved poor soil for Masonry.

Emperor Peter III served as Grand Master of the Russian lodge which was organized in St. Petersburg in 1771. The Russian Orthodox Church expressed its disapproval and Alexander I closed the lodge in 1822. Pierre, in Tolstoy's monumental *War and Peace*, joins this St. Petersburg lodge and later discusses his beliefs with the cynical Prince Andrew: "I myself thought like that and do you know what saved me. Freemasonry. No, don't smile, Freemasonry is not a religious ceremonial sect, as I thought it was. Freemasonry is the best expression of the best, the eternal aspects of humanity." International Communism scorns the bourgeoise pretensions of Masonry; the lodge was outlawed in Soviet Russia in 1922 and post war revivals in such satellites as East Germany have been nipped in the bud. Shortly after World War I the Hungarian Red dictator Bela Kun suppressed the lodge and confiscated its property.

To link Masonry and Communism as allies is an anti-Masonic myth with little substance. Although both oppose the Church and advocate a secular state, they share no common philosophy. The

average middle class American or English Mason rejects the material-
ism, the atheism, the economic interpretation of history, and the
class warfare of Communism as does his Catholic neighbor. Unfortunately, however, the naturalism of the lodge undermines the
basis of the Christian state and thereby renders it vulnerable to
Communism's appeal.

The British exported Freemasonry to India where it captured
the fancy of some of the native princes and the wealthy Parsees.
Rudyard Kipling was initiated at Lahore in 1886 with a Hindu as
Worshipful Master; the other lodge officers included a Moslem,
English Christian, and a Jew. The poet later wrote:

My Mother Lodge

Outside, "Sergeant! Sir! Salute! Salaam!"
Inside — "Brother!" and it doesn't do no 'arm,
We met upon the level an' we parted on the square,
An' I was Junior Deacon in my Mother-Lodge out there!
We 'adn't good regalia,
An' our Lodge was old and bare,
But we knew the Ancient Landmarks,
An' we kept 'em to a hair;
An' lookin' on it backwards
It often strikes me thus,
There ain't such things as infidels
Excep', per'aps, it's us.

Turning to the Western hemisphere, we find about 246,000
Canadian Masons in nine Grand Lodges and small hard cores of
Masons in the Central and South American countries.

Mexican Masonry presents a jumbled picture of schisms and
feuds. Two rival Grand Lodges now claim a combined membership
of 1200 Masons. Novelist Evelyn Waugh describes the role of the
lodge in recent Mexican history:

The first instrument of this policy was Joel Poinsett, who came
to Mexico at the establishment of its independence, first as United
States agent, later as accredited minister; the means he chose, perhaps
the only efficacious means he could have chosen, was the establishment of a rival secret society — the Yorkish rite to oppose the
dominant Scottish Rite. . . .
The Yorkish Rite, introduced by Poinsett, was the natural rallying

point for those who had been disappointed in the shareout of benefits; it was made up of the lawless elements of the Revolution — the Villas and Zapatas of the revolution of 1910 — and was republican, proletarian and fiercely irreligious in character. Five lodges were organized with local chiefs. . . . Soon the two Rites were divided not only by political views but by personal vendettas. For fifty years the history of Mexico becomes a series of coups and plots, assassinations and executions; of embezzlement and bribery; the learned and charitable institutions were sacked to provide funds for rival gangs; the work of three centuries of civilized rule was obliterated in a generation, leaving the nation bankrupt, discredited abroad and divided by irreconcilable hatred at home.[3]

Masonry controlled the government of Guatemala from 1870 to 1945 and left the Church crippled and undermanned. When the late Carlos Castillo Armas overthrew the Communist-dominated government he closed the Grand Lodge as a Communist front but he authorized the house cleaning and reorganization of Guatemalan Masonry. Archbishop Mariano Rossell of Guatemala City reported, "Guatemalan Masonry is actively sectarian. It is opposed to the Church, the clergy, Christianity and all religion. It is determined to exclude the Church and religion from public life."

The largest number of Latin American Freemasons are in Cuba which reports about 17,000. A recent survey conducted by the university section of Catholic Action in Cuba revealed that 3% of the Catholics interviewed admitted membership in the Masonic lodge, 45% said they were not members but would have no objections to joining, and only 3% said they definitely would not become Masons.

Statics for other Latin nations show 5000 Masons in Chile, 2200 in Bolivia, 1200 in Brazil, 650 in Peru, and 550 in Colombia. The role of Latin Masonry in the multitudinous revolutions and social upheavals south of the border would be an involved story. Latins who once would have gravitated toward the lodge as an expression of their discontent now head for more radical social movements.

Since 1920 every president of Chile has been a Mason. In 1958, 75 leading Latin Masons attended the 4th International Masonic Congress in South America held at Santiago. Catholic missionaries

---

[3] Evelyn Waugh, *Robbery Under Law* (London: Chapman and Hall, Ltd., 1939), pp. 126–128.

report complete Masonic domination of the Chilean government, army and public school system.

A joint pastoral letter by the bishops of Argentina in 1959 reminded the faithful that the aims of Catholicism and Freemasonry "are contradictory and absolutely exclude one another." They added that secularism is the "ideological expression proper to Freemasonry."

The only other sizable bodies of Masons are those in Australia and New Zealand where an estimated 365,000 men wear the square and compass. The 10,500 member Grand Lodge of the Philippines also controls the two lodges on Guam. The only Christian nation in the Far East, the Philippines, is represented in the United Nations by a 33rd degree Mason, Francisco Delgado. He also signed the U. N. charter for his country in 1945. The *Nippon Times* (Nov. 13, 1955) reported that two Japanese were initiated into the lodge in the first ceremony conducted entirely in the Japanese language. Several hundred Japanese are now members of lodges largely sponsored by American military authorities.

We are not presenting Masonry as an international conspiracy with well-defined political objectives and secret leaders. We know that the great majority of the world's Masons are American or English bourgeoisie who join the lodge for social or business reasons. World Masonry exhibits the same disunity as world Protestantism and, in fact, Masonry has not yet reached the stage of the embryo World Council of Churches.

Conditions in European Masonry are strikingly different from those in the United States. Masons are few in number and their Masonic identity is seldom known to their neighbors. They never wear lodge jewelry, advertise the time and place of their meetings, or publish names of members or officers. Admittance to the higher degrees is reserved for the most devoted Masons who are selected rather than solicited to progress in the system.

Masons and anti-Masons have often inflated the influence of the lodge in historical events although here and there we have definite proof of Masonic conspiracies. Today even in Latin nations these intrigues are minor annoyances compared to the world-wide conspiracy of international Communism.

CHAPTER XI

OTHER FORBIDDEN SECRET SOCIETIES

Catholics Warned Against Odd Fellows, Knights of Pythias

Three of the dozens of secret societies spawned by Freemasonry were specifically condemned by the Congregation of the Holy Office in 1894. One of the trio, the Sons of Temperance, is now defunct. The other two continue to operate although they have been overshadowed in recent decades by the growth of Masonry in this country.

Sometimes called "poor man's Masonry," the Independent Order of Odd Fellows and the Knights of Pythias lack the members, wealth, influence, and prestige of Masonry. They generally find their members among the working class, farmers, and artisans although office seekers and professional "joiners" may hold membership in Masonry and an assortment of quasi-Masonic associations.

A pastoral letter by Archbishop Katzer of Milwaukee in 1895 outlined the Church's reasons for considering an association unsuitable for the faithful. "The Catholic Church has declared that she considers those societies illicit and forbidden which (1) unite their members for the purpose of conspiring against the State or Church; (2) demand the observance of secrecy to such an extent that it must be maintained even before the rightful ecclesiastical author-

ities; (3) exact an oath from their members or a promise of blind
and absolute obedience; and (4) make use of a ritual and ceremonies
that constitute them sects."

While the penalty for affiliation with the Masonic lodge is excommunication, the penalty for affiliation with the Odd Fellows or
the Knights of Pythias is denial of the sacraments. Once a Catholic
renounces such membership he may resume the full practice of his
faith. As we shall see the obligations administered by these secret
societies are not so objectionable as the Masonic oaths nor have
these societies engaged in the systematic anticlericalism of Masonry.

In fact, in 1896 the Holy Office allowed nominal membership in
the three condemned societies under the following conditions: the
Catholic member entered the society in good faith, his continued
nominal membership would cause no scandal in the community,
he would suffer a grave temporal injury through withdrawal, and
finally no danger of perversion or loss of faith existed. No such
conditions were ever promulgated for nominal membership in the
Masonic lodge. A convert to the Catholic Church or a lapsed Catholic who wishes to return to the faith must sever all Masonic connections. The Catholic Odd Fellow or Knight of Pythias was also
warned by the Holy Office against attending lodge meetings or
frequenting the lodge room. He was asked to pay his dues by mail
or through a third party and under no circumstances was the lodge
authorized to participate in the funeral service.

The earlier 1894 instruction to the American hierarchy had
stated: "The bishops must endeavour by all means to keep the
faithful from joining all and each of the three aforesaid secret
societies, and warn the faithful against them, and if, after proper
monition, they still determine to be members of these societies,
or do not effectually separate themselves from them, they are to be
forbidden the reception of the sacraments."

One reason for the relative leniency in tolerating nominal membership by Catholics in these societies lies in the mutual benefit
features of the Odd Fellows and the Knights. Since its founding
the IOOF has paid out $372,651,644 in benefits to members and

their families while the Knights of Pythias expended $141,764,323.[1] The leading historian of the Odd Fellows movement explains the financial basis of his lodge: "That we require the poorest applicant to contribute as much as the wealthiest, is true, as it is a matter of necessity. Equality in payments is essential not only to equality in benefits but also in feelings. We aim to abolish all considerations of wealth or poverty in our fraternity; to make all feel that as Odd Fellows, at least, they are not only brethren, but equals. He who did not pay an equivalent would feel degraded at receiving benefits, would feel that they were not his just due, but alms."[2]

Catholics who had joined these societies before 1894 or who have joined since in ignorance of the Church's position would be forced to forfeit these financial benefits if they had to break all ties with the lodge.

The heyday of non-Masonic lodges seems to have passed in the United States and few of the scores of such lodges have managed to survive the Great Depression, World War II, television, social security, and low cost group insurance. At one time, for example, the Knights of Pythias claimed 729,000 Knights but the 1957 World Almanac lists only 250,000. Likewise, 50 years ago the 1,330,000 Odd Fellows outnumbered the Masons but today there are almost three Masons for each of the 1,453,731 Odd Fellows.

Like Masonry and unlike Pythian Knighthood, Odd Fellowship is an English creation. Membership in the first recorded lodge (1745) was composed of day laborers and mechanics and the society was obviously patterned after Masonry. The latter, however, appealed to those in the higher social classes and early attracted members of the nobility.

The pioneer Odd Fellow lodges came in for criticism because of their devotion to excessive conviviality and together with other non-Masonic bodies were eventually proscribed by the English government. A group of sober Odd Fellows protested against the drunkenness tolerated in many lodges and formed the Independent

---

[1] *Statistics, Fraternal Societies 1957* (Indianapolis: The Fraternal Monitor, 1957), p. 52.
[2] *Grosh's Manual*, p. 64.

Order of Odd Fellows, Manchester Union (1813) which now represents the majority of Odd Fellows in the British Isles.

An English born coach maker founded the order in this country. Thomas Wildey, a Swedenborgian by religion, had been a member of the parent Grand United Order of Odd Fellows in his native country before settling in Baltimore in 1817. He and four other English immigrants organized the first American lodge in 1819 and kept alive Odd Fellow traditions to such an extent that they were ousted from several taverns which served as meeting places.

Membership was limited to free white males of 21 years or older. "Chinese, Polynesians, Indians, half-breeds and mixed bloods" were specifically excluded from the fraternity as well as women, the deaf, blind, chronically ill and poor. Nevertheless, Grosh's Manual tells us: "Odd Fellowship is a miniature representation among a chosen few of that fraternity which God has instituted among men. Few as are those who represent it, the great principle is wide enough for all. On the broad platform of brotherhood of all nations, parties and sects can meet and freely mingle in offices of needed kindness and mutual well-doing. . . . As all men have God for their father, all are brethren."[3]

Grosh describes the evolution of the order from a simple mutual benefit society to one which engages in religious instruction:

> The order as founded by Brother Wildey was simply a humane institution — its main objects were to relieve the brethren, bury the dead and care for the widow and orphan. But gradually there was infused into its lectures and charges much moral and (unsectarian) religious instruction; and at each revision these principles were increased, and deepened and strengthened, until its beneficial and relief measures, from being ends, have become means to a higher and greater end — to improve and elevate the character of man; to imbue him with conceptions of his capabilities for good; to enlighten his mind; to enlarge the sphere of his affections, and thus to lead him to the cultivation of the true relations designed by the Great Author of his being.[4]

Lodges in Boston and Philadelphia received charters from Baltimore but the growth of the fledgling society was hampered by the

---

[3] Grosh, New Odd Fellow's Manual, p. 109.
[4] Ibid., p. 34.

anti-secret society atmosphere of the Morgan affair. The American Odd Fellows sympathized with the 1813 schism in England and had allied themselves with the protesting Manchester Unity. In 1842 they cut all ties with the Mother Lodge and proclaimed their independence of the Independent Order in England.

That same year to the horror of white Odd Fellows, a group of American Negroes obtained a charter from the original Grand United Order of Odd Fellows. Nevertheless, no one could deny the legitimacy of Negro Odd Fellowship. Nowadays white Odd Fellows deny that this action precipitated the break with the English lodges but, like Masonry, Odd Fellowship draws the line of fellowship between the black and white races.

Since 1880 the Odd Fellows have worked four basic degrees: the initiatory degree and the degrees of friendship, love, and truth. Higher degrees are conferred by Encampments (founded in 1885) and are known as Patriarchal, Golden Rule, and Royal Purple degrees. A military branch, modeled after the Knights Templar, consists of three more degrees and is called the Patriarchs Militant. The solemnity of the lodge itself is relieved by the IOOF's "Shrine" known as the Ancient Order of Samaritans. The chief officer of the local Sanctorum goes by the title "Supreme Monarchos of the Supreme Sanctorum."

In the initiatory degree the candidate is asked: "Do you believe in the existence of a Supreme, Intelligent Being, the Creator and Preserver of the Universe?" Nowhere in the ritual as revised and adopted in St. Paul in 1907 is the name of Christ mentioned nor the subscription to any specifically Christian belief demanded. "No peculiarities of religious belief or practice are requisite to admission into the Order, and none disqualify," according to the 1848 Journal.

Solemn pledges rather than oaths are exacted from the prospective Odd Fellow; the blood curdling penalities of bodily mutilations of Masonry are missing. The initiatory obligation follows:

"I, ——, in the presence of the brothers of the Order now assembled, do solemnly promise that I will never communicate to any one, unless directed to do so by a legal lodge, the signs, tokens or grips, the term, traveling or other passwords belonging to the Independent Order of Odd Fellows. Nor will I expose or lend any of the books or papers relating to the records or secret work of the Order, to any person or persons, except to one specially authorized to receive them. That I will never reveal any private business which may be transacted in my presence in this or any other Lodge. I also promise that I will abide by the laws, rules, and regulations of this Lodge, of the Grand Lodge of the Independent Order of Odd Fellows of (state) or any other Grand or working Lodge to which I may be attached.

"I further promise that I will never wrong a Subordinate or Grand Lodge to the value of anything. Nor will I take part or share, directly or indirectly, in any illegal distribution of funds or other property of the Lodge; but will, to the best of my ability, endeavor to prevent the same. Nor will I wrong a brother or see him wronged without apprising him of approaching danger, if in my power so to do. Should I be expelled or voluntarily leave the Order, I will consider this promise as binding out of it as in it. To the faithful performance of all I pledge my sacred honor."

In the final degree of truth the candidate repeats the following obligation:

"I, ——, in the presence of the members of the Degree of Truth here assembled, do solemnly promise, that I will conceal and never reveal the signs, secrets, and mysteries of this degree, unless it be to a brother Odd Fellow of this degree in good standing, or in a lawful lodge of brothers who shall be legally authorized to receive the same. I furthermore promise to be faithful to my former obligations in this order. To the faithful performance of all which I pledge my sacred honor."

As part of the initiatory degree the candidate is blindfolded, bound in chains, and led around the lodge room to be confronted by a grinning skeleton illuminated by two torches. The Past Grand delivers the charge at initiation which includes the following passage: "With the divisions and classifications of human society our Order holds no fellowship. While it inculcates a veneration for religion and subordination to civil government and its laws, it studiously avoids all affinity with systems of faith or sects, whether religious or political."

The degree of friendship features a playlet of David and Jonathan complete with a representation of Goliath's severed head; the degree of love illustrates the parable of the Good Samaritan (with no reference to the author of the parable). The final Odd Fellow degree is dull even as lodge rituals go. The candidate is simply instructed in the esoteric meanings of the symbols of Odd Fellowship: the all-seeing eye (also a popular Masonic symbol), three links, skull and cross bones, scythe, bow and arrow, quiver and bundle of sticks, ax, heart, globe, ark and serpent, sword, Bible, hour glass and coffin.

By the time of Wildey's death in 1861 the society had grown to 200,000 members and would soon outstrip Masonry as the largest secret society in the country. Baltimore remained the national headquarters and lodges were grouped in separate Grand Lodges for each state. Members included Presidents Grant, Hayes, Garfield, and Harrison.

Fourth of July parades and civic celebrations were enlivened by the appearance of the uniformed Patriarchs Militant after 1882. Clerks and factory workers climbed into their braided and buttoned military coats, adjusted their colorful sashes, donned plumed hats, fastened richly embroidered epaulets, strapped on their trusty swords, and marched down Main Streets throughout the country.

Every Grand Lodge founded one or more homes for aged and indigent members, widows, and orphans, and 54 Odd Fellow homes are now serving the members and their families.

As we have noted, Odd Fellowship failed to hold its own in the United States; the reasons for its decline are not hard to see. The prestige and supposed greater antiquity of Masonry has attracted nearly 4,000,000 American men. Most younger Masons see no particular advantage in joining the Odd Fellows when they might gain more by putting their extra time and funds into the York and Scottish rites. Enlarged social security benefits, union pensions, wider insurance coverage through G.I. insurance and low cost group insurance put the rather modest death benefits of Odd Fellowship in a poor perspective. Finally, the multiplication of all types of other fraternities and clubs has made inroads on the time and interest of prospective lodge members. Three such categories are the several businessmen's service clubs: Rotary, Kiwanis, Lions, Optimist; the various "animal" lodges: Elks, Eagles, and Moose; and the veterans' organizations: American Legion and Veterans of Foreign Wars.

The Daughters of Rebekah, once limited to close female relatives of Odd Fellows, is now open to all single white women over 18 as well as wives, widows, and daughters of Odd Fellows. The Apostolic Delegate in 1907 made the position of the Church plain regarding these auxiliaries: "If these societies are affiliated to societies already nominally condemned by the Church, they fall under the same condemnation, for they form, as it were, a branch of such societies."

The other still active secret society condemned in 1894 is the home grown Knights of Pythias. This society, based on the mythical friendship of the pagan Damon and Pythias, was the creation of Justus H. Rathbone and four other government clerks. Earlier in his career Rathbone had directed a school play centering around the two models of friendship. Rathbone, a Mason and Redman, conceived a lodge ritual exemplifying this friendship and interested his co-workers in the project. The Knights of Pythias was founded in Washington, D. C., in 1861.

The order makes no claims to greater antiquity and occasionally spoofs other societies which feel called upon to claim Adam and Noah as charter members. For example, at the silver anniversary of the Knights, R. L. C. White confessed:

> The actual origin of our Order, as I have said, is definitely known. No mist of antiquity shrouds its inception; no moss of ancient tradition fetters the free and sturdy branches of our Pythian oak. We cannot claim that the founder of our fraternity, coeval with creation, sat in solemn silence on the axis of the universe, and evolved from his inner consciousness the rudimentary principles of a nascent brotherhood as he watched the megatherium gambol in innocent glee on the paleozoic green and the primeval icthyosaurus slowly flap his prehistoric tail.

No tradition tells of any Knight of Pythias who, as assistant architect, carried the antediluvian mortar in a pre-Adamite hod, to help build the Temple of the Sun at Heliopolis; nor is there, in any of our castle halls, a secret coffer wherein is piously preserved an original and authentic lock of hair from the sacred tail of Aaron's golden calf.

Soon after founding the Knighthood Rathbone dropped out of the picture and the infant society faltered. He rejoined and revised his ritual in 1866 and two years later the Knights numbered 3,000. At the request of the Mother Lodge Rathbone was asked to compose the ritual for a new higher degree, the Supreme Order of Pythian Knighthood, but this degree was rejected by the Supreme Lodge which even threatened to excommunicate any Knight who took the degree. Again Rathbone abandoned the society he had founded on the basis of pagan friendship and he remained outside the Castle walls until 1874. After some debate on his fitness to be a Knight he was readmitted and assigned the job of roving lecturer. When he admitted insolvency the Supreme Lodge circulated an appeal for contributions which netted Rathbone $5,085.35.

The Knights followed the lead of the older lodges in refusing admittance to Negroes. Application by a group of Richmond, Va., Negroes was officially denied in 1869 but the applicants maintained that they had been initiated by sympathetic white Knights. They organized the "Knights of Pythias of North and South America, Europe, Asia and Africa" which still survives.

Requirements for white members of the order were sound bodily health and belief in a Supreme Being. Thousands knocked at Castle doors and 31 years after its organization the order claimed 450,000 initiates.

Three basic degrees comprise Pythian Knighthood: Page, Esquire, and Knight. The ritual is remarkably banal and insipid and the modern reader wonders how, even in an age of melodrama and Horatio Alger fiction, such an invention could have stirred men's hearts.

The candidate for the degree of Page repeats his obligation while kneeling before an open coffin containing a skeleton. Two swords on the coffin point toward the neophyte and the Bible rests on the swords.

In the second degree the candidate is tricked into writing the motto of the degree which he has promised to keep secret. The Chancellor Commander takes this opportunity to reprimand the candidate for his offense.

The horseplay of the third degree is reminiscent of college fraternity initiations. The candidate for the degree of Knight is asked to give blind obedience to the Order. To test this obedience the Knights haul out a board of spikes, blindfold the candidate, remove his shoes and command him to leap from a raised platform onto the spikes. Of course, the real board has been removed.

By the time the candidate has reached this third degree he is expected to repeat the following obligation:

"I solemnly promise that I will never reveal the password, grip, signs or any other secret or mystery of this rank, except in a lodge of this order, recognized by and under control of the Supreme Lodge Knights of Pythias of the World, or when being examined by the proper officers of a lodge, or to one whom I shall know to be a member of this rank.

"I further promise that I will not become a member of, recognize or countenance any organization using the name of this order or any derivative thereof, unless recognized by and under the control of the Supreme Lodge Knights of Pythias of the World.

"I further promise that I will always, to the extent of my ability, relieve a worthy knight in distress, endeavor to warn him of any danger which I may know to threaten him or his family, and to aid him whenever and wherever I may be convinced that he is in need.

"I further promise that I will never, by any act of mine voluntarily disturb the domestic relations of a brother knight; but that, so far as possible, I will protect the purity of his household as I would my own.

"I further promise that I will never expose any part of the proceedings of this or any other lodge, nor discuss them in the presence of anyone whom I do not know to be a member of this order.

"I further promise that I will be faithful to my financial obligations to the order; that I will cheerfully and promptly pay all dues and assessments levied by lawful authority and that I will not permit myself to be suspended or expelled for disregard of this law if within my power to prevent.

"I further promise that I will obey the orders of this lodge, of the Grand Lodge having jurisdiction over it, and of the Supreme Lodge Knights of Pythias of the World, and the official mandates of the executive officers thereof.

"To the faithful observance of this obligation I pledge my sacred word of honor. So help me God — and may He keep me steadfast."

Ordinary meetings are opened with prayer by the Prelate: "Supreme Ruler of the Universe, we humbly ask Thy blessing upon the officers and members of this lodge. Aid us to avoid anger and dissension; help us to work together in the spirit of fraternity; and inspire us to exemplify the friendship of Damon and Pythias. Hear and answer us, we beseech Thee. Amen." The name of Jesus Christ is never mentioned lest it scandalize non-Christian Knights.

The playground of Pythian Knighthood, frankly patterned after the Shrine and Grotto, is the Dramatic Order Knights of Khorassan inaugurated in 1894. Allied orders for young people and women are the Junior Order Princes of Jerusalem, Pythian Sisters, and the Sunshine Girls.

President Franklin D. Roosevelt, also a 32nd degree Mason, joined the Knights of Pythias in 1936 in a special initiation in the diplomatic reception room of the White House. His initiation however, hardly offset the loss of 125,000 Knights who bowed out of the order in the course of one biennium during the depression.

The order never managed to establish itself in England or Europe and its lodges are limited to this country, Canada, and Hawaii. About 22 homes for aged Knights are maintained in the United States.

The decline of the Knights of Pythias was hastened by feuds among high ranking officers, court actions, schisms, jealousy, bankruptcy, and depositions. Apparently the example of Damon and Pythias was not enough to inspire the Knights to love their neighbors. The order was also hurt by the same factors in modern American life which we mentioned in our discussion of the IOOF.

The third society listed in the Holy Office's condemnation in 1894 was the Sons of Temperance. Oldest of the many American total abstinence societies, the Sons of Temperance was founded in New York City in 1842 "to reform drunkards and to prevent others from becoming drunkards." It included daughters as well as sons and became one of the few coeducational lodges. By 1907 its membership had dwindled to 14,000 and today the Sons have disappeared from the fraternal scene.

Catholics have been warned against affiliation with a number of other organizations in addition to the Odd Fellows and the Knights of Pythias. The Independent Order of Good Templars was forbidden in 1893; the Holy Office declared in 1917 that it was unlawful to assist in a spiritualistic seance and therefore no Catholics could join a spiritualist society; the Theosophy of Madame Blavatsky and Mrs. Annie Besant was forbidden in a decree in 1919; and the Church forbade membership in the Communist party under pain of grave sin on July 1, 1949.

Obviously many other associations not mentioned by name by the Holy Office are unsuitable for Catholics and other Christians. Organizations which constitute a religious sect, which seek to conspire against Church and State, which demand oaths of blind obedience are condemned by the principles of moral theology. An informed Catholic would therefore steer clear of such societies as the Ku Klux Klan, the Rosicrucians, the Unity School of Christianity, and the Socialist Labor Party even though they have not been singled out by name by the Church.

Two other societies, by no means secret or subversive, have been the subject of recent warnings by Church authorities. The spirit of religious indifference fostered by both organizations might well infect Catholic members and thereby constitutes a threat to their faith. For this reason the Church discourages her children from joining the YMCA or Rotary International.

The YMCA and YWCA, founded and directed by evangelical

Protestants, have succeeded in attracting about one-fourth of their U.S. members from Roman Catholic ranks. Any examination of YMCA reveals a thoroughly Protestant orientation which means that the Church can hardly recommend the organization to Catholic young people. In a circular letter dated Nov. 5, 1920 the Holy Office discussed certain modern organizations:

> Among these associations it will suffice to mention one which is, as it were, the parent of many others, being extremely widespread (especially owing to its valuable relief service during the War), and backed by immense resources, namely the Young Men's Christian Association, or YMCA. It has the undiscerning support, not only of well meaning non-Catholics, who think it salutary to all, or at least harmful to none, but also of some easy-going Catholics who are blind to its true nature. It proclaims its sincere love of youth, as though it had nothing more at heart than to serve their bodily and mental welfare; but at the same time it weakens their faith, under the pretext of purifying it and giving them a better knowledge of the true life "above every church and independently of any religious creed."

A similar word of caution was given in 1950 regarding membership in Rotary, the businessmen's luncheon and service club. Since then Catholic priests have been forbidden to hold membership in Rotary while lay Catholics have been discouraged from joining the 433,000-member club. At the time of the prohibition a number of priests were serving as presidents of local Rotary clubs and a Canadian Catholic held the position of international president. The Holy Office pointed out that Rotary presents a purely natural ethical code without reference to the Church or divine law. Furthermore, in some countries Rotary seems to have become a recruiting service for the Masonic lodges and the center of incipient anti-clerical activities.

The general law of the Church regarding membership of the faithful in lay organizations is summarized in two canons of the Code of Canon Law.

"The faithful are deserving of praise, if they join associations erected, or at least commended by the Church; but they must beware of associations which are secret, condemned, seditious, or suspect, or which seek to evade the legitimate vigilance of the Church" (Canon 684).

"Those who give their names to the Masonic sect, or to other associations of the same kind, which plot against the Church or legitimate civil powers, incur by that very fact an excommunication which is reserved, in a simple manner, to the Holy See" (Canon 2335).

Catholics who understand and value the treasure of their faith will be happy to follow those measures recommended by the Church to preserve this precious gift. Considering the hundreds of associations which bear the approval of the Church or which, at any rate, are neutral and harmless, no Catholic need feel unduly constricted in his social life nor handicapped in his insurance plans by observing the warnings of the Church against a handful of condemned secret societies.

CHAPTER XII

PROTESTANT AND EASTERN ORTHODOX CRITICISM OF MASONRY

Majority of World's Christians Forswear the Lodge

By minimizing the extent of Protestant and Eastern Orthodox opposition to oath-bound secret societies, the Masonic lodge seeks to pose as the champion of non-Catholic Christianity against the encroachments of Rome. The issue then becomes the lodge vs. the Vatican rather than the lodge vs. Christianity.

At least four or five million non-Catholic Christians in the United States belong to denominations which unreservedly forbid affiliation with Masonry and similar secret societies. We are not counting all of the 6,000,000 Lutherans and 2,000,000 Orthodox since some of these Christians belong to bodies which fail to enforce anti-lodge pronouncements. This estimate includes only those who are faced with a choice between lodge membership and church membership. Considering the 475,000,000 Roman Catholics and an estimated 20,000,000 anti-lodge Protestants and Orthodox, we can see that the vast majority of the world's Christians belongs to communions which condemn the lodge for its religion of naturalism, its immoral oaths, and its anti-Christian activities.

The *Lutheran Cyclopedia* explains why Masonry has had the success it has in England and the United States in attracting recruits from the Christian denominations. "Due to the Wesleyan revival in England and the Great Awakening in the United States, with the influence of Protestantism still giving character to national life, Christianity, especially in the United States, was too strong to permit either Freemasonry or Oddfellowship to stress their deistic or anti-Church attitudes. While frankly anti-Christian in its French, German, and Italian branches, Freemasonry in England and the United States has always called itself a supporter of the morality and doctrine of the Protestant Church. Very few candidates realize that they are joining an organization which is essentially antagonistic to the Christian belief in the inspiration of the Bible and the divinity of Jesus Christ."[1]

In essentials Protestants and Orthodox criticize the lodge for the same reasons as do Catholics. Furthermore, Protestants accuse the lodge of advocating salvation by good works rather than by faith alone. They are naturally distressed by the use of mutilated Bible texts in lodge services which delete the name of Jesus Christ and they protest against being yoked with unbelievers in the fellowship of the lodge. The Protestant government of Holland banned Freemasonry in 1735 (three years before the first papal bull on the subject) and the governments of Sweden and Geneva followed suit in 1738. These bans were later lifted.

Pike's opinion of Protestantism was hardly more flattering than his views of Catholicism:

> Catholicism was a vital truth in its earliest ages, but it became obsolete, and Protestantism arose, flourished, and deteriorated. The doctrines of Zoroaster were the best which the ancient Persians were fitted to receive; those of Confucius were fitted for the Chinese; those of Mohammed for the idolatrous Arabs of his age. Each was Truth for the time. Each was a Gospel, preached by a Reformer; and if any men are so little fortunate as to remain content therewith, when others have attained a higher truth, it is their misfortune and not their fault. They are to be pitied for it, and not persecuted.[2]

Not a single distinctively Protestant theological position is upheld by the lodge: total depravity, salvation by faith alone, the priesthood

---

[1] *Lutheran Cyclopedia*, Concordia Publishing House, p. 392.
[2] Albert Pike, *Morals and Dogma*, p. 38.

of all believers, the sole sufficiency of the Bible, or private interpretation of the scriptures. No wonder that those denominations which represent the principles of the Reformation today are vehemently opposed to the lodge.

A number of the most active anti-lodge churches support the work of the National Christian Association, with headquarters at 850 West Madison Street, Chicago, Illinois. This Association, founded in 1868, gathers information about various secret societies and their rituals, publishes the monthly *Christian Cynosure*, distributes thousands of books and tracts warning evangelical Protestants against the seductions of the lodge, and operates a six-man lecture bureau. Chief financial support for the N.C.A. comes from the rapidly-growing Christian Reformed Church, a strict Calvinist body with headquarters in Grand Rapids, Michigan.

Lutheran opposition to Masonry has been spearheaded in this country by the aggressive Lutheran Church-Missouri Synod and by its sister conservative Wisconsin Synod. Together these two orthodox Lutheran bodies enroll more than 2,500,000 Christians and no one may retain membership in the church or approach the communion table who has not renounced the lodge. Most pastors in these synods are better informed on Masonry than the average 32nd degree Mason. They are supplied with up-to-date rituals and anti-lodge materials published and distributed by the Concordia Publishing House of St. Louis.

Every Lutheran synod in the country expresses opposition to oath-bound secret societies in its official statements. Some have undercut their positions by leaving the decision as to whether a particular society constitutes a danger to the Christian faith to the individual conscience. Others prefer moral persuasion to excommunication of those who join lodges and believe they can best demonstrate the Christian ideal by keeping "Christian" Masons in the Church. You will even find pastors of the mildly liberal United Lutheran Church in America who have reached the 32nd degree or who sport the Shriner's crescent.

The Swedish Augustana Synod tolerates membership in the lodge by laymen but never by pastors. Official policy of this 500,000-

member Lutheran body includes the following statement: "They (these synods) agree that a Lutheran Synod should not tolerate pastors who have affiliated themselves with any anti-Christian society. And they admonish their pastors and congregations to testify against the sin of lodgery and to put forth earnest efforts publicly and privately to enlighten and persuade persons who are members of anti-Christian societies to sever their connections with such organizations."

The American Lutheran Church (770,000 members) examines the lodge question in Article 2, Section 4 of its Constitution and By Laws: "This congregation is earnestly opposed to all organizations or societies, secret or open, which, without confessing faith in the Triune God and in Jesus Christ as the eternal Son of the eternal God, incarnate in order to be our only Savior from sin, are avowedly religious and practise forms of religions, teaching salvation by works. It declares such organizations and societies to be anti-Christian and rejects any fellowship with them." At its 1934 meeting this Church declared "a) that the testimony against the lodge dare never cease in our congregations; b) that the treatment of individual lodge members is a matter of Seelsorge (pastoral care)."

These Lutheran bodies and others reflect the hostile attitude of continental Lutheranism toward the Masonic lodge. Every third Protestant in the world is a Lutheran and the weight of Lutheran opposition to the Craft seriously undermines Masonic claims to Protestant approval.

Most Christians in the Holiness and Pentecostal tradition are committed to an unequivocal anti-lodge position. For example, the Constitution and By Laws of the 470,000-member Assemblies of God declares:

> Ours is a last-day message in preparation for the coming of the Lord (Mt. 24:14), leaving us no alternative but wholehearted devotion to the cause of spreading the Gospel (Lk. 9:62), and it is well known that the various secret orders require much valuable time and interest thus diverting the servant of the Lord out of the way (Eph. 5:16).
>
> The nature of such organizations demands secrecy (Jn. 18:20, Acts 26:26) reinforced by unchristian oaths (Mt. 5:34) and strong attachment by binding obligations to persons who are for the most

part unregenerated (2 Cor. 6:14). Moreover, the spirit, philosophy, and general influence of such secret orders aims at the improvement of the natural man only (1 Cor. 2:14; Col. 2:8), thus wrongly channeling by incorrect interpretation important spiritual truths (2 Pet. 3:16).

Confidence in these secret orders and their teachings has always tended toward the embracing of a false hope of salvation through good works and improved moral service (Eph. 2:8, 9).

In consideration of the foregoing, all ministers affiliated with us should refrain from identifying themselves with any of the secret orders which we recognize as essentially of the world, worldly and we advise any who may have identified themselves with such orders to sever their connections therewith (2 Cor. 6:17). Futhermore, our ministers are requested to use their good influence among our lay members to dissuade them from such fraternal affiliations (1 Tim. 4:12; 2 Tim. 2:24–26).

The Church of the Nazarene, a Methodistic denomination of 297,000 members in this country, outlaws lodge membership in its *1956 Manual.* "It is required of all who desire to unite with the Church of the Nazarene, and thus to walk in fellowship with us . . . that they shall evidence this 1) By avoiding evil of every kind, including . . . 7) membership in or fellowship with oath-bound secret orders or fraternities (Article 25)." The attitude of these two denominations, the largest in the Holiness movement, is echoed in official statements by practically all of the many Holiness sects, including the several Churches of God.

When the Christian Reformed Church broke away from the parent Reformed Church in America in 1857, the issue of membership by Christians in the lodge was one of the main points of dispute. Since then the Christian Reformed Church has outstripped the older body and now counts 211,000 adherents. It represents undiluted Calvinism and uncompromising hostility to all secret societies.

Recently the Seventh-Day Adventist Church passed the one million member mark, of whom about 250,000 live in the United States. Adventists cannot join the lodge nor can their theological cousins, the 700,000 Jehovah's Witnesses. Incidentally, the major Protestant denominations which support parochial school systems also head the list of anti-lodge denominations: Missouri and Wisconsin Synod Lutherans, the Christian Reformed, and the Seventh-day Adventists.

Undoubtedly the fastest growing religious movement in modern times, Jehovah's Witnesses flatly forbids membership in the lodge. In a recent issue of their official magazine *Awake!* (circulation 2,625,000) they declare:

> While certain degrees of Freemasonry are limited to those professing to be Christians, there is a striking contrast between what Freemasonry teaches and what the Bible does. Thus Jesus said: "I am the light of the world," but according to Freemasonry a man is a poor, lost, bedarkened soul, even though a dedicated Christian minister, until he is enlightened by Freemasonry. Jesus also said: "I am the way and the truth and the life. No one comes to the Father except through me," but Freemasonry says all religions lead to God. As regards belief and worship, Freemasonry is as inclusive as the Bible is exclusive, Jehovah God demanding "exclusive devotion." On the other hand, as regards members or followers, Christianity is as inclusive — "make disciples of people of all nations" — and welcoming "anyone that wishes" — as Freemasonry is exclusive. It not only forbids proselyting but bars the black race. Two and a half billion persons cannot debar one from becoming a Christian, but just one man bearing a grudge can bar one from becoming a Freemason.[3]

Several Protestant bodies oppose all oaths, even those asked in the courtroom. Naturally they would not consent to the use of an oath in a lodge initiation. They may also have other reasons for warning their members away from the lodge. In this category are the Quakers, Mennonites, and Brethren. A special committee of the Church of the Brethren (197,000) reported on the lodge problem in 1954 and decided "On the basis of information secured from representative pastors and laymen across the Brotherhood, the committee concludes that membership in secret societies involves only a small percentage of our members and creates a serious problem for only a few churches. Yet where such association with secret orders affects the loyalty of members to their church we believe it constitutes enough of a problem that the church should again state its

---

[3] *Awake!* "The History and Nature of Freemasonry," Vol. XXXIX, No. 6, March 22, 1958, p. 24.

conviction that membership in secret, oath-bound orders represents a compromise with secular standards that is unworthy of a consecrated Christian." The United Brethren in Christ (20,000) in their official *Church Handbook* state: "Any member or preacher who shall connect himself with a secret combination shall be regarded as having withdrawn from the church." The executive secretary of the Mennonite General Conference, one of the largest of the 17 Mennonite bodies, wrote the author: "I do not know of any members of our church who belong to a secret order. It has always been made a test of membership. That is, one cannot belong to our church and to a secret order at the same time." Article XIII in the *Statement on Christian Fundamentals*, the Mennonite doctrinal standard, declares, "That secret orders are antagonistic to the tenor and spirit of the Gospel."

John Wesley, founder of Methodism, once commented, "What an amazing banter on all mankind is Freemasonry." However, many of his twentieth-century spiritual children now give allegiance to this banter; some estimates place the percentage of Methodist clergymen who are Masons as high as 90 per cent. English Methodism passed a resolution at the 1927 Bradford Conference which pointed out that, "Freemasonry, in its ritual and official language, is of purely Theistic nature . . . the distinctive faith of Christianity can find no expression in its formulae, and that the Christian message of salvation, through faith in Christ, as the basis alike for home and foreign evangelization, is wholly incompatible with the claims that have been put forward by Freemasons." Although this resolution has never been rescinded, neither has it been strictly enforced. This action by English Methodism was prompted by publication of *The Menace of Freemasonry to the Christian Faith* by the Rev. C. Penney Hunt.

In the United States the main Methodist body has no official objection to dual membership in lodge and church but two smaller Methodist churches deny such dual membership. The *Book of Discipline* of the Free Methodist Church states: "The church condemns secret societies on scriptural grounds and as contrary to the glory of God, and forbids membership in them (paragraph

57.3)." This official church manual explains: "Any society requiring an oath, affirmation, or promise of secrecy, as a condition of membership, is held to be a secret society; and any member joining or continuing in one violates his covenant obligations as set forth in Paragraphs 57, Section 3 and 87, Section 5, and shall in due form be excluded from the church; and the preacher shall report that he is excluded for infraction of our rules and regulations." Likewise, the Wesleyan Methodist Church in its *Discipline* states: "We will on no account tolerate our ministers and members in joining or holding fellowship with Secret Societies, as, in the judgment of the Wesleyan Methodist Church, it is inconsistent with our duties to God to hold such relations (paragraph 57)." The two Methodist bodies enroll a total of 94,000 members and claim to represent the genuine Wesleyan tradition in this country.

Baptist denominations do not legislate for local congregations on any matters including membership in lodges. Consequently most Baptists feel free to join such societies although certain Baptist groups oppose the lodge. For example, the National Representative of the General Association of Regular Baptist Churches (129,000) writes, "I can tell you, however, that the General Association of Regular Baptist Churches, in its moral position is against secret orders. By this I mean that you will find its pastors and most of its members free from connections with secret orders." The writer, Dr. R. T. Ketcham, also forwarded an article on Masonry which he had contributed to the *Baptist Bulletin*, official church journal, and which was reprinted in the *Sunday School Times*.

For many years the strict United Presbyterian Church of North America upheld its ban against the lodge but in 1925 this church declared such membership to be a matter of individual conscience rather than church direction. Since then the United Presbyterians have merged with the northern Presbyterians to form the United Presbyterian Church in the U. S. A. which probably indicates that their historic anti-lodge stand will be further soft-pedaled. The Reformed Presbyterian Church of Ireland, the Free Presbyterian Church of Scotland, and the Orthodox Presbyterian Church of America do not allow dual membership. The latter body established a Committee on Secret Societies which issued a report entitled *Christ or the Lodge?*

The Dutch Reformed Church of South Africa (Cape Synod), which would otherwise find common cause with the *apartheid* policies of Masonry, forbade Masonic membership in 1942.

Within the Church of England a group of Anglo-Catholic priests and laymen raised a furor in 1951 with a proposal to investigate the religious basis of the Masonic order. King George VI, titular head of the Church at that time, and the Archbishop of Canterbury himself were both Masons. One of the leaders of the movement, Dr. Hubert Box, planned to ask for a committee to inquire "whether the theological implications of Freemasonry, as distinct from its benevolent activities, are compatible with the Christian faith as held by the Church." Dr. Box later wrote a penetrating analysis of the lodge entitled *The Nature of Freemasonry.* Another leader of the abortive effort, Walton Hannah, wrote *Darkness Visible* which includes the complete Masonic Blue Lodge ritual as worked in England. A sequel, *Christian by Degrees,* examined the higher Masonic degrees such as the Royal Arch and Rose Croix; its appendix lists by name 17 Anglican bishops and more than 500 priests who hold higher degrees in the Craft. The motion to set up an investigating committee was naturally defeated in the Church Assembly. The Archbishop of York, a non-Mason, rose to declare, "Freemasonry in this country has always avoided the anticlericalism which makes it offensive on the continent. It has never made an attack on Christianity and the Church." Of course, the point at issue was not anticlericalism but naturalism vs. Christianity. The Archbishop then declared that he was reassured about the nature of Freemasonry by the fact that the presiding Archbishop of Canterbury was a Mason and the Grand Master was a prominent Anglican layman.

Relations between the lodge and the Established Church and between the lodge and the crown have always been close and the position of hundreds of Anglican parsons and thousands of laymen would be compromised by any criticism of the Masonic order. Nevertheless, a minority of Anglo-Catholics continue to needle their fellow Anglicans for subscribing to the principles of the naturalistic Masonic sect.

Fundamentalists in the United States generally avoid lodge affiliation even when their churches are officially silent on the subject. The outstanding American evangelist and Oberlin College president, Charles G. Finney, renounced the lodge and wrote *The Character and Claims of Freemasonry* in 1869; it remains a persuasive expose of the anti-Christian orientation of the lodge. Charles A. Blanchard, longtime president of Wheaton College, described Masonry as "a heathen religion grafted onto the stump of a mechanic's guild." Evangelist Dwight L. Moody declared:

> I do not see how any Christian, most of all a Christian minister, can go into these secret lodges with unbelievers. They say they have more influence for good, but I say they can have more influence for good by staying out of them, and then reproving their evil deeds. Abraham had more influence for good in Sodom, although out of it, than Lot had in it. I would rather have ten church members who were separated from the world, than a thousand unseparated members. Come out of the Lodge.

A fundamentalist college such as Wheaton refuses to enroll any student who does not agree to abstain from lodge membership as well as from liquor and tobacco.

General Booth, founder of the Salvation Army, circulated a letter to all Army officers which included the following passage: "No language of mine could be too strong in condemning any officer's affiliation with any Society which shuts Him outside its Temples; and which in its religious ceremonies gives neither Him nor His name any place. . . . As for the future, the Army's views upon this matter will be made known to all who wish to become Officers and acceptance of these views will be necessary before Candidates can be received for training, and further from this time it will be contrary to our regulations for any Officer to join such a Society."

Like Baptist congregations, those in the Churches of Christ fellowship are completely autonomous. The editor of the leading denominational publication, *The Gospel Advocate*, wrote the author, "It is my opinion that the congregations generally would look with disfavor on membership in any secret organization." He added, "Personally I do not belong to any such organization, have never belonged and do not plan to in the future." Membership in the Churches of Christ is estimated at 1,700,000.

Most of the autocephalous Eastern Orthodox churches are critical of the lodge although the largest Orthodox body in this country, the Greek Archdiocese of North and South America, has never issued an official opinion on Freemasonry. The bishops of the Church of Greece, meeting in 1933, unanimously adopted the following statement on Masonry:

> Freemasonry is not simply a philanthropic union or a philosophical school, but constitutes a mystagogical system which reminds us of the ancient heathen mystery-religions and cults — from which it descends and is their continuation and regeneration. This is not only admitted by prominent teachers in the lodges, but they declare it with pride, affirming literally: — "Freemasonry is the only survival of the ancient mysteries and can be called the guardian of them"; "Freemasonry is a direct offspring of the Egyptian mysteries"; "the humble workshop of the Masonic lodge is nothing else than the caves and darkness of the cedars of India and the unknown depths of the Pyramids and the crypts of the magnificent temples of Isis"; "the Greek mysteries of Freemasonry, having passed along the luminous roads of knowledge under the mysteriarchs Prometheus, Dionysius and Orpheus, formulated the eternal laws of the Universe."
>
> Such a link between Freemasonry and the ancient idolatrous mysteries is also manifested by all that is enacted and performed at the initiations. As in the rites of the ancient idolatrous mysteries the drama of the labors and death of the mystery god was repeated, and in the imitative repetition of this drama the initiate dies together with the patron of the mystery religion, who was always a mythical person symbolizing the Sun of nature which dies in winter and is regenerated in spring, so it is also, in the initiation of the third degree, of the patron of Freemasonry Hiram and a kind of repetition of his death, in which the initiate suffers with him, struck by the same instruments and on the same parts of the body as Hiram. According to the confession of a prominent teacher of Freemasonry Hiram is "as Osiris, as Mithra and as Bacchus, one of the personifications of the Sun."
>
> Thus Freemasonry is, as granted, a mystery-religion, quite different, separate, and alien to the Christian faith. This is shown without any doubt by the fact that it possesses its own temples with altars, which are characterized by prominent teachers as "workshops which

cannot have less history and holiness than the Church" and as temples of virtue and wisdom where the Supreme Being is worshipped and the truth is taught. It possesses its own religious ceremonies . . . its own initiations, its own ceremonial ritual, its own hierarchical order and a definite discipline. . . .

It is true that it may seem at first that Freemasonry can be reconciled with every other religion, because it is not interested directly in the religion to which its initiates belong. This is, however, explained by its syncretistic character and proves that in this point also it is an offspring and continuation of ancient idolatrous mysteries which accepted for initiation worshippers of all gods. But as the mystery religions, in spite of the apparent spirit of tolerance and acceptance of foreign gods, leads to a syncretism which undermined and gradually shook confidence in other religions, thus Freemasonry today, which seeks to embrace in itself gradually all mankind and which promises to give moral perfection and knowledge of truth, is lifting itself to the position of a kind of super-religion, looking on all religions (without excepting Christianity) as inferior to itself. Thus it develops in its initiates the idea that only in Masonic lodges is performed the shaping and the smoothing of the unsmoothed and unhewn stone. And the fact alone that Freemasonry creates a brotherhood excluding all other brotherhoods outside it (which are considered by Freemasonry as "uninstructed" even when they are Christian) proves clearly its pretensions to be a super-religion. This means that by Masonic initiation a Christian becomes a brother of the Muslim, the Buddhist, or any kind of rationalist, while the Christian not initiated in Freemasonry becomes to him an outsider.

On the other hand, Freemasonry in prominently exalting knowledge and in helping free research as "putting no limit in the search of truth" (according to its rituals and constitution), and more than this by adopting the so-called natural ethic, shows itself in this sense to be in sharp contradiction with the Christian religion. For the Christian religion exalts faith above all, confining human reason to the limits traced by Divine Revelation and leading to holiness through the supernatural action of grace. In other words, while Christianity, as a religion of Revelation, possessing its rational and super-rational dogmas and truths, asks for faith first, and grounds its moral structure on supernatural Divine Grace, Freemasonry has only natural truth and brings to the knowledge of its initiates free thinking and investigation through reason only. It bases its moral structure only on the natural forces of man, and has only natural aims.

Thus, the incompatible contradiction between Christianity and Freemasonry is quite clear. It is natural that various Churches of other denominations have taken a stand against Freemasonry. Not only has the Western Church branded for its own reasons the

Masonic movement by numerous Papal encyclicals, but Lutheran, Methodist and Presbyterian communities have also declared it to be incompatible with Christianity. Much more has the Orthodox Catholic Church, maintaining in its integrity the treasure of Christian faith, proclaimed against it every time that the question of Freemasonry has been raised. Recently, the Interorthodox Commission which met on Mount Athos and in which the representatives of all the Autocephalous Orthodox Churches took part, has characterized Freemasonry as a "false and anti-Christian system."[4]

His Grace Archbishop Chrysostom of Athens, president of the Assembly of Bishops, concluded:

Freemasonry cannot be at all compatible with Christianity, as far as it is a secret organization, acting and teaching in mystery and secret and deifying rationalism. Freemasonry accepts as its members not only Christians, but also Jews and Muslims. Consequently clergymen cannot be permitted to take part in this association. I consider as worthy of degradation every clergyman who does so. It is necessary to urge upon all who entered it without due thought and without examining what Freemasonry is, to sever all connection with it, for Christianity alone is the religion which teaches absolute truth and fulfills the religious and moral needs of men. Unanimously and with one voice all the Bishops of the Church of Greece have approved what was said, and we declare that all the faithful children of the Church must stand apart from Freemasonry. . . . It is not lawful to belong at the same time to Christ and to search for redemption and moral perfection outside Him. For these reasons true Christianity is incompatible with Freemasonry.

Therefore, all who have become involved in the initiations of Masonic mysteries must from this moment sever all relations with Masonic lodges and activities, being sure that they are thereby of a certainty renewing their links with our one Lord and Savior which were weakened by ignorance and by a wrong sense of values. The Assembly of Bishops of the Church of Greece expects this particularly and with love from the initiates of the lodges, being convinced that most of them have received Masonic initiation not realizing that by it they were passing into another religion, but on the contrary from ignorance, thinking that they had done nothing contrary to the faith of their fathers.[5]

Mormonism appropriated features of the Masonic ritual for its own temple rites, especially the endowment ceremony. This cere-

---

[4] Quoted by Walton Hannah, *Darkness Visible*, pp. 70–73.
[5] Quoted by Walton Hannah, *op. cit.*, pp. 73–74.

mony in which young Mormons are introduced to the esoteric aspects of the cult includes secret passwords, grips, and a Masonic type apron embroidered with fig leaves. Both Joseph Smith and his successor Brigham Young were Masons and the Mormon lodges at Nauvoo, Illinois, initiated as many as 1,500 Mormon Masons in a single year. Later both Smith and Young were expelled from the Masonic order and the charters for the Nauvoo lodges were withdrawn by the Grand Lodge of Illinois. When the Grand Master in Nevada issued a dispensation for a Utah lodge in 1865 he stipulated that this lodge exclude all Mormons. "You will take notice, that Mormons claiming to be Masons be excluded from the right of visiting, and also that petitions for the degrees of Masonry shall not be received from any person who is known to be a Mormon," he directed. This Utah lodge was later dissolved and not re-established until 1872.

Today Utah Masons refuse to initiate members of the Church of Jesus Christ of Latter Day Saints fearing domination of the Grand Lodge by Mormons. Likewise the Mormon priesthood prefers not to encourage membership in the lodge lest the faithful realize the extent of lodge borrowings in secret church rites and lest they divide their loyalties between church and lodge. A handful of Mormons residing outside of Utah have entered Masonic lodges from which their religious leaders were once ousted.

Considering the many Christian denominations, Catholic, Protestant, and Eastern Orthodox, which have taken a positive stand against Masonry, we may ask why all Christian bodies have not adopted similar policies. In the first place, denominations in the liberal or modernist Protestant tradition may see no conflict between their interpretation of Christianity as primarily an ethical system and the religion of naturalism of the lodge. They skirt the central issue of Christ's divinity and deny the inspiration of the Bible; Christianity for them is not the exclusive faith which other Christians recognize. Among the churches in this category we find the Congregationalists, Unitarians, many Methodists, Universalists, and Disciples of Christ.

Second, many Protestant bodies organized with a congregational polity take no stand on other doctrinal issues and therefore should not be expected to take a stand on the lodge. They recognize no authority over the local congregation. The Baptist churches, for example, comprise the largest Protestant family in the United States and a national statement on secret societies, pro or con, would be considered affrontery on the part of the loosely organized national denominations.

Third, some denominations have apparently swallowed the fable that the rituals and teachings of Masonry are secret and that consequently no investigation may be successfully undertaken by an outside agency. Of course, anyone who has done research in this area can testify that authentic lodge rituals are easily procured and that extensive libraries of materials are available to responsible researchers. Denominations which have witnessed against the lodge for decades, such as the Lutheran Church-Missouri Synod and the Christian Reformed Church, have compiled materials on Masonry which they would undoubtedly share with committees appointed by other Christian churches.

Finally, we must conclude that some large denominations are so infiltrated by Masonic ministers and dependent on Masonic benefactors that they lack the courage to call for an investigation of the lodge question. A genuine investigation of the problem by the huge Methodist Church or the Presbyterian or Protestant Episcopal Churches is quite remote. Nevertheless, individual pastors often entertain private reservations about the compatibility of Masonry and Christianity and may decline solicitations to affiliate and discourage active church members who seek their counsel in this matter.

On the other hand, many Protestants receive counsel such as the following which appeared in a recent issue of *Look* Magazine. A distraught wife had written Dr. Norman Vincent Peale to say that her husband had joined a lodge and that she now feels she has lost his confidence and has been cut out of his life. She declared she had never believed in secret organizations. Dr. Peale replied:

> As a fraternal-organization member, I can assure you that you should be glad of your husband's membership. Such lodges teach the highest standards of conduct and are creative influences. There

is no "secret" that isn't good. Since most fraternal orders are founded on the Bible, the "secrets" are all there. Relax and have a sense of humor. Don't you know that all men are boys and like a gang, especially if there are jokes and passwords and such paraphernalia? Don't let jealousy and insecurity become a barrier between your husband and you. Why not join the women's auxiliary such fraternal orders usually have, and have a few "sisters" and "secrets" yourself? You'll have lots of fun.[6]

Where Protestant denominations with Masonic sympathies predominate in a community such as in the South or in many rural areas, the local Masonic lodge often takes on the appearance of an interfaith men's fellowship. The vigorous opposition of other Protestants and of Orthodox and Catholic Christians is ignored or unknown.[7] This situation is confined to England and the United States; where Grand Orients represent Masonry the conflict between lodge and church for the Christian's loyalty is unknown. "The problem of a Freemason who is also a member of a Christian Church, be it Catholic, Orthodox or Protestant, does not really arise in France," writes Marius Lepage in Le Symbolisme, June-July, 1953.

What is significant is that the great majority of the world's Christians see the lodge as the cultic expression of naturalism and as such a rival to the Christian faith. Furthermore, as Hannah points out, "No Church that has seriously investigated the religious teachings and implications of Freemasonry has ever yet failed to condemn it."[8] It becomes Masonry's public relations task to squelch any moves for such an investigation on the part of other Protestant denominations and to belittle the considerable opposition to the lodge by non-Catholic Christians.

---

[6] Look Magazine, April 1, 1958, p. 60.

[7] The latest development in Protestant-Masonic relations is the decision of the United Lutheran Church in America, largest U. S. Lutheran body, to bar Masons from ordination to the ministry and to refuse ministers permission to join the lodge. ULCA ministers who now hold membership will be allowed to continue their pastorates but are encouraged to drop their dual church-lodge membership. This move was demanded by the other three Lutheran communions which are planning to enter a merger with the ULCA by 1960.

[8] Walton Hannah, Darkness Visible, p. 78.

CHAPTER XIII

CHRISTIANITY AND THE LODGE

Jesus Christ or Hiram Abiff?

When a Catholic abandons his faith and joins the Masonic sect the Church recognizes his switch of allegiance and considers him excommunicated. The Church would be untrue to her divine commission if she were to turn her back and pretend that her sons can serve two masters. Protestant churches which acknowledge the exclusive claims of Jesus Christ and the religious basis of the lodge follow a similar course.

We believe that anyone who has followed our discussion to this point will agree that this is the only course of action which a Christian denomination can pursue. The Masonic lodge may avoid anticlerical activities in certain nations, may support commendable charitable undertakings, may disclaim its own religious orientation. Nevertheless the Christian knows that he cannot worship the Triune God on Sunday morning and the Grand Architect on lodge night. He knows he cannot participate in religious worship with non-Christians praying to T.G.A.O.T.U. and still observe Christ's command to ask the Father in His name.

Masonic friends may assure us that the lodge itself does not bar Catholics from membership and that nothing detrimental to the Church has ever been voiced in their Temples. This may very well be true, but it is quite beside the point. Christians do not feel free to become Buddhists simply because Buddhists may refrain from attacking Christianity. They do not become Buddhists or Moslems because Christ, not Buddha or Mohammed, is the Way, the Truth, and the Life.

For all Masonry cares the Bible might never have been written, the Second Person of the Blessed Trinity never have become man or died for man's sins, never have instituted the sacraments or established a Church. Masonry relegates these to the categories of "sectarian" and "peculiar" dogmas and those who believe in them are warned not to drag them into the Temples of Masonry's universal religion. Masonry carries man back to a pre-Christian reliance on human reason alone with absolutely no reference to the Christian revelation. We readily admit that a belief in God and in the immortality of the soul is better than atheism. Masonry, however, does not labor to convert twentieth-century atheists and agnostics to theism; the lodge offers Christian men a pre-Christian religious worship, theology, and morality.

What possible advantages would a Christian see in the lodge which would induce him to deny the claims of Jesus Christ and seek admission into Masonry? We find a number of such advantages dangled before prospective members of the lodge but none of these withstand examination.

In the first place, the lodge promises to make its initiates privy to great secrets. They will be "in" while the rest of mankind, including most of Christendom, will sit in the darkness outside. Nowhere does Masonry promise more and deliver less; the great secrets of the lodge are neither great nor secret. Are these the secrets of the universe? Are these secrets too blinding in brilliance for the minds of women, children, and the "profane"? Are they the keys to spiritual, physical, and mental happiness? Alas, they consist of a few passwords and secret grips and ritual mumbo jumbo. The dissatisfied Master Mason must be enticed by the carrot of higher and higher degrees to find the secrets he expected in the Blue Lodge. He never does.

What is more, the secrets for which he has paid in the coin of the realm and in hours of fruitless memorization are not even secret. He should have known that real secrets in a mass organization of 4,100,000 men are illusory. Anyone with curiosity about the subject can easily procure all the genuine Masonic rituals he wishes. Recently, a friend of the author, a rabbi, complained that he had wasted evening after evening deciphering the King Solomon's code book for his Blue Lodge initiation and did not find out until later that he could have purchased the ritual in plain English at a bookstore a few blocks from the Masonic Temple. It happens that publishers and vendors of Masonic books, like their profane colleagues, are in business to make money and not to preserve inconsequential lodge secrets.

Other candidates for the lodge are attracted by the promise of preference. Once they become eligible to wear the Masonic ring or lapel button certainly their business will pick up, they will sell more life insurance, they will gain more patients or clients. Perhaps if they get into legal difficulties they will find a brother Mason on the bench or in the jury box. And should they decide to run for public office they will enjoy the electoral support of their brethren of the white apron.

A minute's analysis will destroy this illusion. In many communities, particularly in the Eastern part of the country, the Mason who flaunts his affiliation may well antagonize as many customers and voters as he expects to win. In many Southern communities where most white Protestant bourgeoisie are already members, he cannot expect such preferential treatment since most of his competitors also wear the square and compass. Elsewhere the Mason may find some doors open to him which would have otherwise remained shut and he may pick up a few votes which would have gone to the opposition candidate. He would be foolish to think, however, that more than a handful of Americans make it a practice to investigate lodge membership in their complex daily activities. Will the 32nd degree Mason who sells tainted meat or weighs his thumb with the pork chops continue to attract his lodge brothers to his shop? Will the bleeding victim of the highway accident seek the proper password from the physician who comes to his aid? Will the Mason be happy to pay $100 extra to buy his next Ford from the Worshipful Master? Will General Motors or RCA pay a higher dividend to stockholders who belong to the lodge? And do normal people stop to debate: "Between two men of equal ability, I will choose the one who belongs to the same lodge as I do." No one need fear that if he gives a good haircut, sells merchandise of quality, writes readable magazine articles, serves a tasty meal he will suffer in his business relationships because he lacks a Masonic pin.

We do not wish to deprecate Masonic benevolence, another so called advantage to membership, but we feel we should again stress that there is no comparison between the charity of the Christian churches and that of the lodge. While the lodge carefully limits its disbursements to those who are paid up members, the Church extends her charity to all: men and women, young and old, white and black. The lodge takes pains to exclude women, children, Negroes, the poor, crippled, and senile from its Temples. The only ones who are accepted for Masonic membership are those who are most unlikely ever to need charitable assistance. "If ye love them that love you, what thanks have ye? Do not even the publicans the same?" Anyone so foolish as to rely on the lodge for help in adversity would do better to put his dues and assessments into insurance, annuities, common stocks, bonds, bank deposits, or real estate. During a serious depression Masons desert the lodge by the hundreds of thousands and the average of $3 per member per year for charity drops to pennies. On the other hand, one who is looking for opportunities to serve his fellow man need not look for them in the lodge. He can find abundant opportunities in his church, in youth work, in service clubs, and in similar groups.

Good fellowship is another promise which the lodge makes its candidates and we will not deny that such fellowship flourishes in many lodges. It should. Practically all the members fall into the same social class: white, Protestant, bourgeois. Such jarring topics as religion and politics are outlawed. "Nonconformists" may be disposed of by means of the black ball. Again, what a difference between the exclusive lodge and the all embracing Church of

Christ which turns no one from her doors. What no one can seriously propose, however, is that any man looking for companionship must find it in the Masonic lodge. Even the smallest country village supports dozens of clubs and social organizations which fill man's gregarious needs. A person can choose a church society such as the Holy Name Society or Legion of Mary, a veterans' organization such as the VFW or the American Legion, a service club such as the Lions or Kiwanis, a trade union, and a bewildering assortment of bridge and poker clubs, P.T.A.'s, discussion groups, Catholic Action organizations, square dance groups, stamp clubs, etc.

Finally, some men are wooed into the lodge by simple vanity, by the opportunity to claim grandiose titles, to command a respect that they do not find in their own homes or in their occupations. Some find an escape from an oppressively feminine social life in the all-male lodge.[1]

Although we believe that Masonry ultimately undermines the Christian basis of society, propagates an insidious religion of naturalism and the spirit of religious indifference, administers an immoral oath, and often engages in or tolerates anticlericalism, we

---

[1] "The fraternal orders reached their peak of popularity in the 1920's, when most of the adult males of America belonged to one or more. Their secrecy and rituals and costumes may seem a bit juvenile today, but these orders did make one important contribution to democracy. Like the Roman Catholic Church, they embraced the span of the American social order. The lodge hall was an excellent place for people of all classes to become acquainted, and to understand each other's problems and aspirations. Such an opportunity to make oneself known to people of the superior class is an essential precondition to winning acceptance into their class, in case one has ambitions. The fraternal orders performed, at least, that vital function of providing a common ground for intermingling. A generation ago in Jonesville, W. Lloyd Warner points out, "every important man in the community was a Mason, and often an Odd Fellow or a Woodman," And the man who managed to become a high-degree Mason was taking a long, sure stride toward social success. Today, the situation has changed abruptly not only in Jonesville but throughout America. The members of the two upper classes have abandoned the lodges almost completely in favor of their exclusive civic-type groups; and typically, the lower classes have not been able to follow them into these. Nowadays, the Masons and the Knights of Columbus draw their membership predominately from the limited-success class; and the Woodmen of the World, the Odd Fellows, Eagles, and Redmen draw a very large part of their membership from the workingman class. Even among the three lower classes the fraternal orders have lost much of their fascination." Vance Packard, The Status Seekers (New York, David McKay Co., 1959, pp. 192–193).

have a Christian obligation to love Masons. When we deny the compatibility of the lodge and the Christian faith we do not question the sincerity of Protestant Masons but their consistency. It seems that many of us reveal a lack of consistency in many areas of our lives. We are scientific about one subject and superstitious about another. We harbor mutually incompatible political and economic theories but we compartmentalize our lives so that our inconsistencies do not show.

Catholics along with many Protestant and Eastern Orthodox know of the basic incompatibility of Church and lodge because this has long been demonstrated by their religious leaders. We pray that those who receive no such guidance from their churches in this matter will investigate for themselves the mutually exclusive claims of Jesus Christ and the Grand Architect. "That all men should honor the Son, even as they honor the Father. He that honoreth not the Son honoreth not the Father who hath sent Him" (Jn. 5:23).

Not the Grand Architect of the Universe but God the Father, the Son, and the Holy Spirit is our God. Not Hiram Abiff but Jesus Christ is our Saviour. Not by the mock death and resurrection rite of the Master Mason's degree but by the sacrament of baptism do we become children of God and heirs of heaven.

APPENDIX

HUMANUM GENUS

ENCYCLICAL LETTER OF OUR HOLY FATHER
BY DIVINE PROVIDENCE

Pope Leo XIII

ON

FREEMASONRY

To Our Venerable Brethren, All Patriarchs, Primates,
Archbishops and Bishops of the Catholic World,
In Grace and Communion with the Apostolic See,

Pope Leo XIII

Venerable Brethren, Health and Apostolic Benediction

The race of man, after its miserable fall from God, the Creator and the Giver of heavenly gifts, "through the envy of the devil," separated into two diverse and opposite parts of which the one steadfastly contends for truth and virtue, the other for those things which are contrary to virtue and to truth. The one is the kingdom of God on earth, namely, the true Church of Jesus Christ; and those who desire from their heart to be united with it, so as to gain salvation, must of necessity serve God and His only-begotten Son with their whole mind and with an entire will. The other is the kingdom of Satan, in whose possession and control are all who follow the fatal example of their leader and of our first parents, those who refuse to obey the divine and eternal law, and who have many aims of their own in contempt of God, and many aims also against God.

This twofold kingdom St. Augustine keenly discerned and described after the manner of two cities, contrary in their laws because striving for contrary objects; and with a subtle brevity he expressed the efficient

169

cause of each in these words: "Two loves formed two cities: the love of self, reaching even to contempt of God, an earthly city; and the love of God, reaching to contempt of self, a heavenly one." At every period of time each has been in conflict with the other, with a variety and multiplicity of weapons, and of warfare, although not always with equal ardor and assault. At this period, however, the partisans of evil seem to be combining together, and to be struggling with united vehemence, led on or assisted by that strongly organized and widespread association called the Freemasons. No longer making any secret of their purposes, they are now boldly rising up against God Himself. They are planning the destruction of holy Church publicly and openly, and this with the set purpose of utterly despoiling the nations of Christendom, if it were possible, of the blessings obtained for us through Jesus Christ our Saviour. Lamenting these evils, We are constrained by the charity which urges Our heart to cry out often to God: "For lo, Thy enemies have made a noise; and they that hate Thee have lifted up the head. They have taken a malicious counsel against Thy people, and they have consulted against Thy saints. They have said, 'Come, and let us destroy them, so that they be not a nation.' "

In so urgent a crisis, when so fierce and so pressing an onslaught is made upon the Christian name, it is Our office to point out the danger, to mark who are the adversaries, and to the best of Our power to make head against their plans and devices, that those whose salvation is committed to Us may not perish, and that the kingdom of Jesus Christ intrusted to Our charge may not only stand and remain whole, but may be enlarged by an ever-increasing growth throughout the world.

The Roman Pontiffs Our predecessors, in their incessant watchfulness over the safety of the Christian people, were prompt in detecting the presence and the purpose of this capital enemy immediately it sprang into the light instead of hiding as a dark conspiracy; and moreover they took occasion with true foresight to give the alarm, as it were, and to admonish both princes and nations to stand on their guard and not allow themselves to be caught by the devices and snares laid out to deceive them.

The first warning of the danger was given by Clement XII in the year 1738, and his Constitution was confirmed and renewed by Benedict XIV. Pius VII followed the same path; and Leo XII, by his Apostolic Constitution, "Quo graviora," put together the acts and decrees of former Pontiffs on this subject, and ratified and confirmed them forever. In the same sense spoke Pius VIII, Gregory XVI, and many times over Pius IX.

For as soon as the constitution and the spirit of the Masonic sect were clearly discovered by manifest signs of its actions, by cases investigated, by the publication of its laws, and of its rites and commentaries, with the addition often of the personal testimony of those who were in the secret, this Apostolic See denounced the sect of the Freemasons, and publicly declared its constitution, as contrary to law and right, to be pernicious no less to Christendom than to the State; and it forbade any one to enter the society, under the penalties which the Church is wont to inflict upon exceptionally guilty persons. The sectaries, indignant at this, thinking to elude or to weaken the force of these decrees, partly by contempt of them and partly by calumny, accused the Sovereign Pontiffs who had passed them either of exceeding the bounds of moderation in their decrees or of decreeing what was not just. This was the way in which they endeavored to elude the authority and the weight of the Apostolic Constitutions of Clement XII and Benedict XIV, as well as of Pius VII and Pius IX. Yet in the very society itself there were to be found men who unwillingly acknowledged that the Roman Pontiffs had acted within their right, according to the Catholic doctrine and discipline. The Pontiffs received the same assent, and in strong terms, from many princes and heads of governments, who made it their business either to delate the Masonic society to the Apostolic See, or of their own accord by special enactments to brand it as pernicious, as, for example, in Holland, Austria, Switzerland, Spain, Bavaria, Savoy, and other parts of Italy.

But, what is of highest importance, the course of events has demonstrated the prudence of Our predecessors. For their provident and paternal solicitude had not always and everywhere the result desired; and this, either because of the simulation and cunning of some who were active agents in the mischief, or else because of the thoughtless levity of the rest who ought, in their own interest, to have given to the matter their diligent attention. In consequence the sect of Freemasons grew with a rapidity beyond conception in the course of a century and a half, until it came to be able, by means of fraud or of audacity, to gain such entrance into every rank of the State as to seem to be almost its ruling power. This swift and formidable advance has brought upon the Church, upon the power of princes, upon the public well-being, precisely that grievous harm which Our predecessors had long before foreseen. Such a condition has been reached that henceforth there will be grave reason to fear, not indeed for the Church — for her foundation is much too firm to be overturned by the effort of men — but for those States in which prevails the power, either of the sect of which we are speaking or of other similar sects which lend themselves to it as disciples and subordinates.

For these reasons We had no sooner come to the helm of the Church than We clearly saw and felt it to be Our duty to use Our authority to the very utmost against so vast an evil. Several times already, as occasion warranted, We have attacked certain chief points of teaching which showed in a special manner the perverse influence of Masonic opinions. Thus, in Our Encyclical Letter, "Quod Apostolici muneris,"

We endeavored to refute the monstrous doctrines of the Socialists and Communists; afterwards, in another beginning "Arcanum," We took pains to defend and explain the true and genuine idea of domestic life, of which marriage is the spring and origin; and again, in that which begins "Diuturnum," We described the ideal of political government conformed to the principles of Christian wisdom, which is marvelously in harmony, on the one hand, with the natural order of things, and, on the other, with the well-being of both sovereign princes and of nations. It is now Our intention, following the example of Our predecessors, directly to treat of the Masonic society itself, of its whole teaching, of its aims, and of its manner of thinking and acting, in order to bring its power for evil more and more into the light, and to do what We can to arrest the contagion of this fatal plague.

There are several organized bodies which, though differing in name, in ceremonial, in form and origin, are nevertheless so bound together by community of purpose and by the similiarity of their main opinions, as to make in fact one thing with the sect of the Freemasons, which is a kind of center whence they all go forth, and whither they all return. Now, these no longer show a desire to remain concealed; for they hold their meetings in the daylight and before the public eye, and publish their own news organs; and yet, when thoroughly understood, they are found still to retain the nature and the habits of secret societies. There are many things like mysteries which it is the fixed rule to hide with extreme care, not only from strangers, but from very many members also; such as their secret and final designs, the names of the chief leaders, and certain secret and inner meetings, as well as their decisions, and the ways and means of carrying them out. This is, no doubt, the object of the manifold difference among the members as to right, office, and privilege — of the received distinction of orders and grades, and of that severe discipline which is maintained.

Candidates are generally commanded to promise — nay, with a special oath, to swear — that they will never, to any person, at any time or in any way, make known the members, the passes, or the subjects discussed. Thus, with a fraudulent external appearance, and with a style of simulation which is always the same, the Freemasons, like the Manichees of old, strive, as far as possible, to conceal themselves, and to admit no witnesses but their own members. As a convenient manner of concealment, they assume the character of literary men and scholars associated for purposes of learning. They speak of their zeal for a more cultured refinement, and of their love for the poor; and they declare their one wish to be the amelioration of the condition of the masses, and to share with the largest possible number all the benefits of civil life. Were these purposes aimed at in real truth, they are by no means the whole of their object. Moreover, to be enrolled, it is necessary that the candidates promise and undertake to be thenceforward strictly obedient to their leaders and masters with the utmost submission and fidelity, and to be ready to do their bidding upon the slightest expression of their will; or, if disobedient, to submit to the direst penalties and death itself. As a fact, if any are judged to have betrayed the doings of the sect or to have resisted commands given, punishment is inflicted on them not infrequently, and with so much audacity and dexterity that the assassin very often escapes the detection and penalty of his crime.

But to simulate and wish to lie hid; to bind men like slaves in the very tightest bonds, and without giving any sufficient reason; to make use of men enslaved to the will of another for any arbitrary act; to arm men's right hands for bloodshed after securing impunity for the crime — all this is an enormity from which nature recoils. Wherefore reason and truth itself make it plain that the society of which we are speaking is in antagonism with justice and natural uprightness. And this becomes still plainer, inasmuch as other arguments also, and those very manifest, prove that it is essentially opposed to natural virtue. For, no matter how great may be men's cleverness in concealing and their experience in lying, it is impossible to prevent the effects of any cause from showing, in some way, the intrinsic nature of the cause whence they come. "A good tree cannot produce bad fruit, nor a bad tree produce good fruit." Now, the Masonic sect produces fruits that are pernicious and of the bitterest savor. For, from what We have above most clearly shown, that which is their ultimate purpose forces itself into view — namely, the utter overthrow of that whole religious and political order of the world which the Christian teaching has produced, and the substitution of a new state of things in accordance with their ideas, of which the foundations and laws shall be drawn from mere "Naturalism."

What We have said, and are about to say, must be understood of the sect of the Freemasons taken generically, and in so far as it comprises the associations kindred to it and confederated with it, but not of the individual members of them. There may be persons among these, and not a few, who, although not free from the guilt of having entangled themselves in such associations, yet are neither themselves partners in their criminal acts, nor aware of the ultimate object which they are endeavoring to attain. In the same way, some of the affiliated societies, perhaps, by no means approve of the extreme conclusions which they would, if consistent, embrace as necessarily following from their common principles, did not their very foulness strike them with horror. Some of these, again, are led by circumstances of times and places either to aim at smaller things than the others usually attempt, or than they themselves would wish to attempt. They are not, however, for this reason, to be reckoned as alien to the Masonic federation; for the Masonic federation is to be judged not so much by the things which it has done, or brought to completion, as by the sum of its pronounced opinions.

Now, the fundamental doctrine of the Naturalists, which they sufficiently make known by their very name, is that human nature and human reason ought in all things to be mistress and guide. Laying this down, they care little for duties to God, or pervert them by erroneous and vague opinions. For they deny that anything has been taught by God; they allow no dogma of religion or truth which cannot be understood by the human intelligence, nor any teacher who ought to be believed by reason of his authority. And since it is the special and exclusive duty of the Catholic Church fully to set forth in words truths divinely received, to teach, besides other divine helps to salvation, the authority of its office, and to defend the same with perfect purity, it is against the Church that the rage and attack of the enemies are principally directed.

In those matters which regard religion let it be seen how the sect of the Freemasons acts, especially where it is more free to act without restraint, and then let any one judge whether in fact it does not wish to carry out the policy of the Naturalists. By a long and persevering labor, they endeavor to bring about this result — namely, that the office and authority of the Church may become of no account in the civil State; and for this same reason they declare to the people and contend that Church and State ought to be altogether disunited. By this means they reject from the laws and from the commonwealth the wholesome influence of the Catholic religion; and they consequently imagine that States ought to be constituted without any regard for the laws and precepts of the Church.

Nor do they think it enough to disregard the Church — the best of guides — unless they also injure it by their hostility. Indeed, with them it is lawful to attack with impunity the very foundations of the Catholic religion, in speech, in writing, and in teaching; and even the rights of the Church are not spared, and the offices with which it is divinely invested are not safe. The least possible liberty to manage affairs is left to the Church; and this is done by laws not apparently very hostile, but in reality framed and fitted to hinder freedom of action. Moreover, We see exceptional and onerous laws imposed upon the clergy, to the end that they may be continually diminished in number and in necessary means. We see also the remnants of the possessions of the Church fettered by the strictest conditions, and subjected to the power and arbitrary will of the administrators of the State, and the religious orders rooted up and scattered.

But against the Apostolic See and the Roman Pontiff the contention of these enemies has been for a long time directed. The Pontiff was first, for specious reasons, thrust out from the bulwark of his liberty and of his right, the civil princedom; soon he was unjustly driven into a condition which was unbearable because of the difficulties raised on all sides; and now the time has come when the partisans of the sects openly declare, what they have plotted for a long time in secret among themselves, that the sacred power of the Pontiffs must be abolished, and that the Pontificate itself, founded by divine right, must be utterly destroyed. If other proofs were wanting, this fact would be sufficiently disclosed by the testimony of well informed men, of whom some at other times, and others again recently, have declared it to be true of the Freemasons that they especially desire to assail the Church with irreconcilable hostility, and that they will never rest until they have destroyed whatever the supreme Pontiffs have established for the sake of religion.

If those who are admitted as members are not commanded to abjure the Catholic doctrines by any form of words, this omission, so far from being contrary to the designs of the Freemasons, is more useful for their purposes. First, in this way they easily deceive the simple-minded and the heedless, and can induce a far greater number to become members. Again, as all who offer themselves are received whatever their form of religion, they thereby teach the great error of this age — that regard for religion should be held as an indifferent matter, and that all religions are alike. This manner of reasoning is calculated to bring about the ruin of all forms of religion, and especially of the Catholic religion, which, as it is the only one that is true, cannot, without great injustice, be regarded as merely equal to other religions.

But the Naturalists go much further; for having, in the highest things, entered upon a wholly erroneous course, they are carried headlong to extremes, either by reason of the weakness of human nature, or because God inflicts upon them the just punishment of their pride. Hence it is that they no longer consider as certain and permanent those things which are fully understood by the natural light of reason, such as certainly are — the existence of God, the immaterial nature of the human soul, and its immortality. The sect of the Freemasons, by a similar course of error, is exposed to these same dangers; for although in a general way they may profess the existence of God, they themselves are witnesses that they do not all maintain this truth with the full assent of the mind or with a firm conviction. Neither do they conceal that this question about God is the greatest source and cause of discords among them; in fact, it is certain that a considerable contention about this same subject has existed among them very lately. But indeed the sect allows great liberty to its votaries, so that to each side is given the right to defend its own opinion, either that there is a God, or that there is none; and those who obstinately contend that there is no God are as easily initiated as those who contend that God exists, though, like the Pantheists, they have false notions concerning Him: all which is nothing else than taking away the reality, while retaining some absurd representation of the divine nature.

When this greatest fundamental truth has been overturned or weakened, it follows that those truths also which are known by the teaching of nature must begin to fall — namely, that all things were made by the free will of God the Creator; that the world is governed by Providence; that souls do not die; that this life of men upon the earth will be followed by another and an everlasting life.

When these truths are done away with, which are as the principles of nature and important for knowledge and for practical use, it is easy to see what will become of both public and private morality. We say nothing of those more heavenly virtues, which no one can exercise or even acquire without a special gift and grace of God; of which necessarily no trace can be found in those who reject as unknown the redemption of mankind, the grace of God, the sacraments, and the happiness to be obtained in heaven. We speak now of the duties which have their origin in natural probity. That God is the Creator of the world and its provident Ruler; that the eternal law commands the natural order to be maintained, and forbids that it be disturbed; that the last end of men is a destiny far above human things and beyond this sojourning upon the earth: these are the sources and these the principles of all justice and morality.

If these be taken away, as the Naturalists and Freemasons desire, there will immediately be no knowledge as to what constitutes justice and injustice, or upon what principle morality is founded. And, in truth, the teaching of morality which alone finds favor with the sect of Freemasons, and in which they contend that youth should be instructed, is that which they call "civil," and "independent," and "free," namely, that which does not contain any religious belief. But how insufficient such teaching is, how wanting in soundness, and how easily moved by every impulse of passion, is sufficiently proved by its sad fruits, which have already begun to appear. For wherever, by removing Christian education, the sect has begun more completely to rule, there goodness and integrity of morals have begun quickly to perish, monstrous and shameful opinions have grown up, and the audacity of evil deeds has risen to a high degree. All this is commonly complained of and deplored; and not a few of those who by no means wish to do so are compelled by abundant evidence to give not infrequently the same testimony.

Moreover, human nature was stained by original sin, and is therefore more disposed to vice than to virtue. For a virtuous life it is absolutely necessary to restrain the disorderly movements of the soul, and to make the passions obedient to reason. In this conflict human things must very often be despised, and the greatest labors and hardships must be undergone, in order that reason may always hold its sway. But the Naturalists and Freemasons, having no faith in those things which we have learned by the revelation of God, deny that our first parents sinned, and consequently think that free will is not at all weakened and inclined to evil. On the contrary, exaggerating rather our natural virtue and excellence and placing therein alone the principle and rule of justice, they cannot even imagine that there is any need at all of a constant struggle and a perfect steadfastness to overcome the violence and rule of our passions.

Wherefore we see that men are publicly tempted by the many allurements of pleasure; that there are journals and pamphlets with neither moderation nor shame; that stage-plays are remarkable for license; that designs for works of art are shamelessly sought in the laws of a so-called realism; that the contrivances of a soft and delicate life are most carefully devised; and that all the blandishments of pleasure are diligently sought out by which virtue may be lulled to sleep. Wickedly also, but at the same time quite consistently, do those act who do away with the expectation of the joys of heaven, and bring down all happiness to the level of mortality, and, as it were, sink it in the earth. Of what We have said the following fact, astonishing not so much in itself as in its open expression, may serve as a confirmation. For since generally no one is accustomed to obey crafty and clever men so submissively as those whose soul is weakened and broken down by the domination of the passions, there have been in the sect of the Freemasons some who have plainly determined and proposed that, artfully and of set purpose, the multitude should be satiated with a boundless license of vice, as, when this had been done, it would easily come under their power and authority for any acts of daring.

What refers to domestic life in the teaching of the Naturalists is almost all contained in the following declarations. That marriage belongs to the genus of commercial contracts, which can rightly be revoked by the will of those who made them, and that the civil rulers of the State have power over the matrimonial bond; that in the education of youth nothing is to be taught in the matter of religion as of certain and fixed opinion; and each one must be left at liberty to follow, when he comes of age, whatever he may prefer. To these things the Freemasons fully assent; and not only assent, but have long endeavored to make them into a law and institution. For in many countries, and those nominally Catholic, it is enacted that no marriages shall be considered lawful except those contracted by the civil rite; in other places the law permits divorce; and in others every effort is used to make it lawful as soon as may be. Thus the time is quickly coming when marriages will be turned into another kind of contract — that is, into changeable and uncertain unions which fancy may join together, and which the same when changed may disunite.

With the greatest unanimity the sect of the Freemasons also endeavors to take to itself the education of youth. They think that they can easily mold to their opinions that soft and pliant age, and bend it as they will; and that nothing can be more fitted than this to enable them to bring up the youth of the State after their own plan. Therefore in the education and instruction of children they allow no share either of teaching or of discipline to the ministers of the Church; and in many places they have procured that the education of youth shall be exclusively in the hands of laymen, and that nothing which treats of the most important and most holy duties of men to God shall be introduced into the instructions on morals.

Then come their doctrines of politics, in which the Naturalists lay down that all men have the same right, and are in every respect of equal and like condition; that each one is naturally free; that no one has the right to command another; that it is an act of violence to require men to obey any authority other than that which is obtained from themselves. According to this, therefore, all things belong to the free people; power is held by the command or permission of the people, so that, when the popular will changes, rulers may lawfully be deposed; and the source of all rights and civil duties is either in the multitude or in the governing authority when this is constituted according to the latest doctrines. It is held also that the State should be without God; that in the various forms of religion there is no reason why one should have precedence of another; and that they are all to occupy the same place.

That these doctrines are equally acceptable to the Freemasons, and that they would wish to constitute States according to this example and model, is too well known to require proof. For some time past they have openly endeavored to bring this about with all their strength and resources; and in this they prepare the way for not a few bolder men who are hurrying on even to worse things, in their endeavor to obtain equality and community of all goods by the destruction of every distinction of rank and property.

What therefore the sect of the Freemasons is, and what course it pursues, appears sufficiently from the summary We have briefly given. Their chief dogmas are so greatly and manifestly at variance with reason that nothing can be more perverse. To wish to destroy the religion and the Church which God Himself has established, and whose perpetuity He insures by His protection, and to bring back after a lapse of eighteen centuries the manners and customs of the pagans, is signal folly and audacious impiety. Neither is it less horrible nor more tolerable that they should repudiate the benefits which Jesus Christ has mercifully obtained, not only for individuals, but also for the family and for civil society, benefits which, even according to the judgment and testimony of enemies of Christianity, are very great. In this insane and wicked endeavor we may almost see the implacable hatred and spirit of revenge with which Satan himself is inflamed against Jesus Christ. So also the studious endeavor of the Freemasons to destroy the chief foundations of justice and honesty, and to co-operate with those who would wish, as if they were mere animals, to do what they please, tends only to the ignominious and disgraceful ruin of the human race.

The evil, too, is increased by the dangers which threaten both domestic and civil society. As We have elsewhere shown, in marriage, according to the belief of almost every nation, there is something sacred and religious; and the law of God has determined that marriages shall not be dissolved. If they are deprived of their sacred character and made dissoluble trouble and confusion in the family will be the result, the wife being deprived of her dignity and the children left without protection as to their interests and well-being. To have in public matters no care for religion, and in the arrangement and administration of civil affairs to have no more regard for God than if He did not exist, is a rashness unknown to the very pagans; for in their heart and soul the notion of a divinity and the need of public religion were so firmly fixed that they would have thought it easier to have a city without foundation than a city without God. Human society, indeed, for which by nature we are formed, has been constituted by God the Author of nature; and from Him, as from their principle and source, flow in all their strength and permanence the countless benefits with which society abounds. As we are each of us admonished by the very voice of nature to worship God in piety and holiness, as the Giver unto us of life and of all that is good therein, so also and for the same reason, nations and States are bound to worship Him; and therefore it is clear that those who would absolve society from all religious duty act not only unjustly but also with ignorance and folly.

As men are by the will of God born for civil union and society, and as the power to rule is so necessary a bond of society that, if it be taken away, society must at once be broken up, it follows that from Him who is the Author of society has come also the authority to rule; so that whosoever rules, he is the minister of God. Wherefore, as the end and nature of human society so requires, it is right to obey the just commands of lawful authority, as it is right to obey God who ruleth all things; and it is most untrue that the people have it in their power to cast aside their obedience whensoever they please.

In like manner, no one doubts that all men are equal one to another, so far as regards their common origin and nature, or the last end which each one has to attain, or the rights and duties which are thence derived. But as the abilities of all are not equal, as one differs from another in the powers of mind or body, and as there are very many dissimilarities of manner, disposition, and character, it is most repugnant to reason to endeavor to confine all within the same measure, and to extend complete equality to the institutions of civil life. Just as a perfect condition of the body results from the conjunction and composition of its various members, which, though differing in form and purpose, make, by their union and the distribution of each one to its proper place, a combination beautiful to behold, firm in strength, and necessary for use; so, in the commonwealth, there is an almost infinite dissimilarity of men, as parts of the whole. If they are to be all equal, and each is to follow his own will, the State will appear most deformed; but if, with a distinction of degrees of dignity, of pursuits and employments, all aptly conspire for the common good, they will present a natural image of a well-constituted State.

Now, from the disturbing errors which We have described the greatest dangers to States are to be feared. For, the fear of God and reverence for divine laws being taken away, the authority of rulers despised, sedition permitted and approved, and the popular passions urged on to lawlessness, with no restraint save that of punishment, a change and overthrow of all things will necessarily follow. Yea, this change and overthrow is deliberately planned and put forward by many associations of Communists and Socialists; and to their undertakings the sect of Freemasons is not hostile, but greatly favors their designs, and holds in common with them their chief opinions. And if these men do not endeavor to carry out their extreme views at once and everywhere, it is not to be attributed to their teaching and their will, but to the virtue of that divine religion which cannot be destroyed; and also because the sounder part of men, refusing to be enslaved to secret societies, vigorously resist their insane attempts.

Would that all men would judge of the tree by its fruits, and would acknowledge the seed and origin of the evils which press upon us, and of the dangers that are impending! We have to deal with a deceitful and crafty enemy, who, gratifying the ears of people and of princes, has ensnared them by smooth speeches and by adulation. Ingratiating themselves with rulers under a pretense of friendship, the Freemasons have endeavored to make them their allies and powerful helpers for the destruction of the Christian name; and that they might more strongly urge them on, they have, with determined calumny, accused the Church of invidiously contending with rulers in matters that affect their authority and sovereign power. Having insured their own safety and audacity by these artifices, they have begun to exercise great weight in the government of States; nevertheless they are prepared to shake the foundations of empires, to harass the rulers of the State, to accuse, and to cast them out, as often as they appear to govern otherwise than they themselves could have wished. In like manner they have deluded the people by flattery. Proclaiming liberty and public prosperity with a loud voice, and saying that it was owing to the Church and to sovereigns that the multitude were not drawn out of their unjust servitude and poverty, they have imposed upon the people; and, exciting them by a thirst for novelty, they have urged them to assail both the Church and the civil power. Nevertheless, the expectation of the benefits which were hoped for was greater than the reality; indeed, the common people, more oppressed than they were before, are deprived in their misery of that solace which, if things had been arranged in a Christian manner, they would have had with ease and in abundance. But whoever strive against the order which divine Providence has constituted usually pay the penalty of their pride, and meet with affliction and misery where they rashly hoped to find all things prosperous and in conformity with their desires.

The Church, if she directs men to render obedience chiefly and above all to God the sovereign Lord, is wrongly and falsely believed either to be envious of the civil power or to arrogate to herself something of the rights of sovereigns. On the contrary, she teaches that what is rightly due to the civil power must be rendered to it with a conviction and consciousness of duty. In teaching that from God Himself comes the right of ruling, she adds a great dignity to civil authority, and no small help toward obtaining the obedience and good-will of the citizens. The friend of peace and sustainer of concord, she embraces all with maternal love; and, intent only upon giving help to mortal man, she teaches that to justice clemency must be joined, equity to authority, and moderation to law-giving; that no one's right must be violated; that order and public tranquillity are to be maintained; and that the poverty of those who are in need is, as far as possible, to be relieved by public and private charity. "But for this reason," to use the words of St. Augustine, "men think, or would have it believed, that Christian teaching is not suited to the good of the State; for they wish the State to be founded not on solid virtue, but on the impunity of vice." Knowing these things, both princes and people would act with political wisdom, and according to the needs of general safety, if, instead of joining with Freemasons to destroy the Church, they joined with the Church in repelling their attacks.

Whatever the future may be, in this grave and widespread evil it is Our duty, Venerable Brethren, to endeavor to find a remedy. And because We know that Our best and firmest hope of a remedy is in the power of that divine religion which the Freemasons hate in proportion to their fear of it, We think it to be of chief importance to call that most saving power to Our aid against the common enemy. Therefore, whatever the Roman Pontiffs Our predecessors have decreed for the purpose of opposing the undertakings and endeavors of the Masonic sect, and whatever they have enacted to deter or withdraw men from societies of this kind, We ratify and confirm it all by Our Apostolic authority; and trusting greatly to the good-will of Christians, We pray and beseech each one, for the sake of his eternal salvation, to be most conscientiously careful not in the least to depart from what the Apostolic See has commanded in this matter.

We pray and beseech you, Venerable Brethren, to join your efforts with Ours, and earnestly to strive for the extirpation of this foul plague, which is creeping through the veins of the State. You have to defend the glory of God and the salvation of your neighbor; and with this object of your strife before you, neither courage nor strength will be wanting. It will be for your prudence to judge the means by which you can best overcome the difficulties and obstacles you meet with. But as it befits the authority of Our office that We Ourselves should point out some suitable way of proceeding, We wish it to be your rule first of all to tear away the mask from Freemasonry, and to let it be seen as it really is; and by sermons and pastoral letters to instruct the people as to the artifices used by societies of this kind in seducing men and enticing them into their ranks, and as to the depravity of their opinions and the wickedness of their acts. As Our predecessors have many times repeated, let no man think that he may for any reason whatsoever join the Masonic sect, if he values his Catholic name and his eternal salvation as he ought to value them. Let no one be deceived by a pretense of honesty. It may seem to some that Freemasons demand nothing that is openly contrary to religion and morality; but, as the whole principle and object of the sect lies in what is vicious and criminal, to join with these men or in any way to help them cannot be lawful.

Further, by assiduous teaching and exhortation, the multitude must be drawn to learn diligently the precepts of religion; for which purpose We earnestly advise that by opportune writings and sermons they be taught the elements of those sacred truths in which Christian philosophy is contained. The result of this will be that the minds of men will be made sound by instruction, and will be protected against many forms of error and inducements to wickedness, especially in the present unbounded freedom of writing and insatiable eagerness for learning.

Great, indeed, is the work; but in it the clergy will share your labors, if, through your care, they are fitted for it by learning and a well-trained life. This good and great work requires to be helped also by the industry of those among the laity in whom a love of religion and of country is joined to learning and goodness of life. By uniting the efforts of both clergy and laity, strive, Venerable Brethren, to make men thoroughly know and love the Church; for the greater their knowledge and love of the Church, the more will they be turned away from clandestine societies.

Wherefore, not without cause do We use this occasion to state again what We have stated elsewhere, namely, that the Third Order of St. Francis, whose discipline We prudently mitigated a little while ago should be studiously promoted and sustained: for the whole object of this Order, as constituted by its founder, is to invite men to an imitation of Jesus Christ, to a love of the Church, and to the observance of all Christian virtues; and therefore it ought to be of great influence in suppressing the contagion of wicked societies. Let, therefore, this holy sodality be strengthened by a daily increase. Among the many benefits to be expected from it will be the great benefit of drawing the minds of men to liberty, fraternity, and equality of right; not such as the Freemasons absurdly imagine, but such as Jesus Christ obtained for the human race and St. Francis aspired to: the liberty, We mean, of sons of God, through which we may be free from slavery to Satan or to our passions, both of them most wicked masters; the fraternity whose origin is in God, the common Creator and Father of all; the equality which, founded on justice and charity, does not take away all distinctions among men, but, out of the varieties of life, of duties, and of pursuits, forms that union and that harmony which naturally tend to the benefit and dignity of the State.

In the third place, there is a matter wisely instituted by our forefathers, but in course of time laid aside, which may now be used as a pattern and form of something similar. We mean the associations or guilds of workmen, for the protection, under the guidance of religion, both of their temporal interests and of their morality. If our ancestors, by long use and experience, felt the benefit of these guilds, our age perhaps will feel it the more by reason of the opportunity which they will give of crushing the power of the sects. Those who support themselves by the labor of their hands, besides being, by their very condition, most worthy above all others of charity and consolation, are also especially exposed to the allurements of men whose ways lie in fraud and deceit. Therefore they ought to be helped with the greatest possible kindness, and to be invited to join associations that are good, lest they be drawn away to others that are evil. For this reason, We greatly wish, for the salvation of the people, that, under the auspices and patronage of the Bishops, and at convenient times, these guilds may be generally restored. To Our great delight, sodalities of this kind and also associations of masters have already been established in many places, having, each class of them, for their object to help the honest workman, to protect and guard his children and family, and to promote in them piety, Christian knowledge, and a moral life. And in this matter We cannot omit mentioning that exemplary society, named after its founder, St. Vincent, which has deserved so well of the people of the lower order. Its acts and its aims are well known. Its whole object is to give relief to the poor and miserable. This it does with singular prudence and modesty; and the less it wishes to be seen, the better is it fitted for the exercise of Christian charity and for the relief of suffering.

In the fourth place, in order more easily to attain what We wish, We commend to your fidelity and watchfulness in a special manner the young, as being the hope of human society. Devote the greatest part of your care to their instruction; and do not think that any precaution can be great enough in keeping them from masters and schools whence the pestilent breath of the sects is to be feared. Under your guidance, let parents, religious instructors, and priests having the cure of souls, use every opportunity, in their Christian teaching, of warning their children and pupils of the infamous nature of these societies so that they may learn in good time to beware of the various and fraudulent artifices by which their promoters are accustomed to ensnare people. And those who instruct the young in religious knowledge will act wisely if they induce all of them to resolve and to undertake never to bind themselves to any society without the knowledge of their parents or the advice of their parish priest or director.

We well know, however, that our united labors will by no means suffice to pluck up these pernicious seeds from the Lord's field, unless the Heavenly Master of the vineyard shall mercifully help us in our endeavors. We must, therefore, with great and anxious care, implore of Him the help which the greatness of the danger and of the need requires. The sect of the Freemasons shows itself insolent and proud of its success, and seems as if it would put no bounds to its pertinacity. Its followers, joined together by a wicked compact and by secret counsels, give help one to another, and excite one another to an audacity for evil things. So vehement an attack demands an equal defense — namely, that all good men should form the widest possible association of action and of prayer. We beseech them, therefore, to stand together with united hearts, and unmoved against the advancing force of the sects; and in mourning and supplication to stretch out their hands to God, praying that the Christian name may flourish and prosper, that the Church may enjoy its needed liberty, that those who have gone astray may return to a right mind, that error at length may give place to truth, and vice to virtue. Let us take as our helper and intercessor the Virgin Mary, Mother of God, so that she, who from the moment of her conception overcame Satan, may show her power over these evil sects, in which is revived the contumacious spirit of the demon, together with his unsubdued perfidy and deceit. Let us invoke Michael, the prince of the heavenly angels, who drove out the infernal foe; and Joseph, the spouse of the Most Holy Virgin, and heavenly Patron of the Catholic Church; and the great apostles, Peter and Paul, the fathers and victorious champions of the Christian faith. By their patronage, and by perseverance in united prayer, We hope that God will mercifully and opportunely succor the human race, which is encompassed by so many dangers.

As a pledge of heavenly gifts and of Our benevolence, We lovingly grant in the Lord, to you, Venerable Brethren, and to the clergy and all the people committed to your watchful care, Our Apostolic Benediction.

Given at St. Peter's in Rome, the twentieth day of April, 1884, the 6th year of Our Pontificate.

LEO XIII, POPE.

BIBLIOGRAPHY

The Ancient Arabic Order of the Nobles of the Mystic Shrine for North America (Chicago: Ezra A. Cook, 1921).

Beharrell, T. G., Odd Fellows Monitor and Guide (Indianapolis: Robert Douglass, 1894).

Blanchard, Charles A., Modern Secret Societies (Chicago: National Christian Association, 1938).

Box, Hubert S., The Nature of Freemasonry (London: Augustine Press, 1952).

Cahill, E., Freemasonry and the Anti-Christian Movement (Dublin: M. H. Gill & Son., 1952).

Carlile, Richard, Manual of Freemasonry (London: William Reeves).

Carnahan, James R., Pythian Knighthood, Its History and Literature (Cincinnati: Pettibone, 1892).

Dillon, George E., Freemasonry Unmasked (London: Britons, 1956).

Duncan, Malcolm C., Duncan's Masonic Ritual and Monitor (Rev.) (Chicago: Ezra A. Cook, 1952).

Durrah, Delmar Duane, History and Evolution of Freemasonry (Chicago: Charles T. Powner Co., 1951).

Fahey, Denis, The Kingship of Christ and Organized Naturalism (Dublin: Holy Ghost Missionary College, 1949).

Ferguson, Charles W., Fifty Million Brothers (New York: Farrar and Rinehart, 1937).

Finney, Charles G., Character and Claims of Freemasonry (Chicago: National Christian Association, 1948).

Graebner, Theodore, A Handbook of Organizations (St. Louis: Concordia Publishing House, 1948).

——— Is Masonry a Religion? (St. Louis: Concordia Publishing House, 1946).

Grosh, A. B., New Odd Fellows (New York: Maynard, Merrill & Co., 1895).

Gruber, Herman, Article entitled "Masonry" in Catholic Encyclopedia.

Hannah, Walton, Darkness Visible (London: Augustine Press, 1952).

——— Christian by Degrees (London: Augustine Press, 1954).

Haywood, H. L., Freemasonry and Roman Catholicism (Chicago: Masonic History Co., 1943).

——— The Great Teachings of Masonry (New York: George H. Doran, 1923).

Haywood, H. L., and Craig, James E., A History of Freemasonry (New York: John Day Co., 1927).

Johnson, Humphrey J. T., Freemasonry: A Short Historical Sketch (London: Catholic Truth Society, 1952).

Jones, Bernard E., Freemasons' Guide and Compendium (London: George G. Harrap, 1950).

Kurth, Karl, The Lodge (St. Louis: Concordia Publishing House).

Lepper, J. Herron, Famous Secret Societies (London: Sampson, Low, Marston & Co., 1938).

Macdonald, Fergus, The Catholic Church and the Secret Societies in the United States (New York: United States Catholic Historical Society, 1946).

MacEss, Jay, Why Blame the Masons? (New York: Paulist Press, 1928).

Mackey, Albert G., Lexicon of Freemasonry (New York: Maynard, Merrill & Co., 1871).

———— Masonic Ritualist (New York: Clark & Maynard, 1869).

———— Symbolism of Freemasonry, rev. by Robert I. Clegg (Chicago: Masonic History Co., 1946).

———— Encyclopedia of Freemasonry (Philadelphia: L. H. Everts, 1887).

———— A Text Book of Masonic Jurisprudence (New York: Maynard, Merrill & Co., 1859).

Macoy, Robert, Masonic Burial Services with General Instructions (Chicago: Ezra A. Cook, 1954).

McReavy, Lawrence L., Forbidden and Suspect Societies (London: Catholic Truth Society, 1956).

Malloy, Joseph I., May Catholics be Masons? (New York: Paulist Press).

Miller, D. F., and Doherty, J. E., Why Catholics Can Not be Freemasons (Liguori, Mo.: Liguorian Pamphlet Office, 1954).

Morgan, William, Freemasonry Exposed (Batavia, N. Y.: 1827).

Newton, Joseph Fort, The Builders (Cedar Rapids, Iowa: The Torch Press, 1915).

Nickel, Theodore F., and Manz, James G., A Christian View of Freemasonry (St. Louis Concordia Publishing House, 1957).

Pick, Fred L., and Knight, G. Norman, The Pocket History of Freemasonry (New York: Philosophical Library, 1953).

Pike, Albert, Morals and Dogma (Charleston, S. C.: Supreme Council of the Thirty-third degree for the Southern Jurisdiction of the United States, 1881).

Preuss, Arthur, A Dictionary of Secret and Other Societies (St. Louis: B. Herder Book Co., 1924).

———— A Study in American Freemasonry, 2nd ed. (St. Louis: B. Herder Book Co., 1908).

Quigley, Joseph A. M., Condemned Societies (Washington, D. C.: Catholic University of America, 1927).

Revised Knights of Pythias (Chicago: Ezra A. Cook, 1914).

Revised Knight Templarism (Chicago: Ezra A. Cook, 1944).

Revised Odd Fellowship (Chicago: Ezra A. Cook, 1951).

Rice, John R., *Lodges Examined by the Bible* (Wheaton, Ill.: Sword of the Lord Publishers, 1943).

Ronayne, Edmond, *The Master's Carpet* (Chicago: Ezra A. Cook, 1879).

————— *Ronayne's Handbook of Freemasonry* (Chicago: Ezra A. Cook, 1955).

Rosen, Peter, *The Catholic Church and Secret Societies* (Milwaukee: Houkamp & Cannon, 1902).

Rumble, L., *Catholics and Freemasonry* (St. Paul, Minn.: Radio Replies Press).

Scotch Rite Masonry, Illustrated (Chicago: Ezra A. Cook, 1953), 2 vols.

Secret Societies Illustrated (Chicago: Ezra A. Cook).

Sibley, W. G., *The Story of Freemasonry* (Gallipolis, Ohio: The Lion's Paw Club, 1904).

Statistics, Fraternal Societies 1957 (Indianapolis: The Fraternal Monitor, 1957).

Stevens, Albert C., *The Cyclopaedia of Fraternities* (New York: E. B. Treat and Co., 1907).

Stillson, Henry Leonard, *History of the Ancient and Honorable Fraternity of Free and Accepted Masons and Concordant Orders* (Boston: Fraternity Publishing Co., 1912).

Van Cott, Charles, *Freemasonry, a Sleeping Giant* (Minneapolis: T. S. Denison & Co., 1959).

"Vindex," *Light Invisible, the Freemason's Answer to Darkness Visible* (London: Regency Press, 1952).

Voorhis, Harold V. B., *Masonic Organizations and Allied Orders and Degrees* (Red Bank, N. J.: Henry Emmerson, 1952).

Ward, J. S. M., *The Masonic Why and Wherefore* (London: Baskerville Press, 1929).

Webster, Nesta H., *Secret Societies and Subversive Movements* (London: Britons, 1955).

Williamson, Harry A., *The Prince Hall Primer* (Chicago: Ezra A. Cook, 1957).

INDEX

Acacia fraternity, 118
"Acacian," meaning of, 78
Acacia plant, 44
Adams, John Quincy, on Masonry, 5
affaire des fiches, 124 f
Allegory, Masonic, 2
Altar, Masonic, 76
Amaranth, Order of, 117
American Lutheran Church, and
Masonry, 150
American rite, 67; see also York rite
American University, and Scottish rite,
66
Ancient and Accepted Rite, English,
55, 58
Ancient Arabic Order Nobles of the
Mystic Shrine, see Shrine
Ancient and Honorable Guild of the
Leather Apron, 118
Ancient Order of Samaritans (IOOF),
137
Anderson, Dr. James, 15 f
Anglican Church, and Masonry, 155 f
Anglicans, Masonic, 122
Anglo-Catholics, and Masonry, 155 f
Anti-Catholicism, Knight Kadosh, 61;
among Masons, 2; and Masonry,
88 ff
Anticlericals, and Masonry, 17
"Antients," formation of, 17; ritual of,
22
Anti-Masonic party, 9
Anti-Semitism, German Masonic, 3,
125
Apron, Masonic, 31, 36
Argentina, bishops of, 132
Aristocracy, English, and Masonry, 15 f;
see also England, Masonry in
Assemblies of God, and Masonry, 150
Ataturk, Kemal, and Masonry, 129
Atheism, Albert Pike on, 108
Atheists, and Masonry, 4
Attendance, lodge, 6

Augustana Synod, Lutheran, and Ma-
sonry, 149 f
Australia, Masonry in, 132
Austria, Masonry in, 126
Awake!, on Masonry, 152

Ballot, membership, 20
Baptism, Masonic, 77
Baptist churches, and Masonry, 154,
161
Baylor University, and Scottish rite, 66
Bela Kun, and Hungarian Masonry,
129
Belgium, Masonry in, 126
Benedict XIV, Pope, and Masonry,
104, 107
Benefits, Knights of Pythias, 135;
IOOF, 134 f
Benevolence, Masonic, 11 f, 166
Bible, in lodge, 22; Masonic, 76 f; Ma-
sonic attitude toward, 77
Bishops, Anglican Masonic, 155
Blake, Eugene Carson, and tax ex-
emption of church property, 91
Blakemore, Louis B., on "higher" de-
grees, 54
Blanchard, Charles A., on Knight
Kadosh degree, 65; on Masonry, 156
Blazing Star, interpretation of, 80 f
Blue Friars, Society of, 118
Blue Lodge, 19, 57; basic Masonry, 6,
53; Masonry confined to, 110
Blue Lodges, number of, 6; and reli-
gion, 88
Boaz, 31
Bolivia, Masonry in, 131
Bonaparte, Joseph, and Grand Orient,
123; and Masonry in Spain, 126
Book of Constitutions, on religion, 16
Books, Scottish rite, and religion, 95
Booth, William, General, on Masonry,
156

189

McGill, John, Bishop, on Masonry, 105
Mackey, Albert G., on altar in Masonry, 76; on Masonry and religion, 73 f, 80; on Scottish rite degrees, 57; on shock of entrance, 77
McLoughlin, Emmett, and Masons, 96
"Ma-hah-bone," 48; in Masonic legend, 67
Maria Theresa, and Austrian Masonry, 104, 126
Marquess of Ripon, conversion to Church, 122
Marshall, George, Mason, 5
Martin Luther film, New Age on, 93
Masonic word, grand, 48
Masonry, Anglo-Saxon, 17; attraction of, 9 f; Catholic origin of, 15; and Christianity, 71; Christian objections to, 101; de-Christianization of, 17; definition of, 2; European, 120 ff; founding of, 3; French, 55; in French revolution, 123; Latin and European, 120 ff; Negro, 10; origin of, 13 ff; Orthodox opposition to, 147; Protestant opposition to, 147 ff; speculative, 3, 15; supposed advantages of, 164 ff
Masons, American, number of, 1; operative, and Masonry, 14 f; 32nd degree, 110
Master Mason, degree, 19; initiation, 38 ff
Mazzini, Mason, 105
Membership, Masonic, means of attaining, 19; nominal, in condemned societies, 134
Mennonites, and Oaths, 152 f
Methodism, and Masonry, 153
Methodists, 160
Mexico, Masonry in, 130 f
Military organization, Masonic, 117 f
Minors, and Masonry, 4
Missouri Synod, see Lutheran Church — Missouri Synod
"Moderns," 17; ritual of, 22
Moody, Dwight L., on Masonry, 156
Morals and Dogma, by Albert Pike, 56
Morgan, William, case of, and Masons, 8 f
Morin, Stephen, 55
Mormonism, and Masonry, 159 f
Moslems, and Masonry, 16; and Scottish rite, 59; symbols, in Shrine, 111
Mussolini, Benito, and Masonry, 128
Mystic Order of Veiled Prophets of the Enchanted Realm, see Grotto, Veiled Prophets

Napoleon I, and Masonry, 123
National Christian Association, and Masonry, 149
National Grange, and Masonry, 9
National Sojourners, 117 f
The Nature of Freemasonry, 155
Nazis, Austrian, and Masonry, 126; and Masons, 125
Negroes, and Masonry, 4, 10 f, 118
New Age, 2; anti-Catholicism of, 66; and Catholicism, 89 ff
Newman clubs, New Age on, 94 f
New Zealand, Masonry in, 132
Nixon, Richard, New Age and, 91
Norway, Masonry in, 126

Oath, Christian view of, 82; Entered Apprentice, 28 f; Fellow Craft, 35 f; Knight Kadosh, 62 f; Knights of Pythias, 142 f; Master Elect of Fifteen, 59; Master Mason, 40 f; IOOF degree of truth, 138 f; Protestant opposition to, 152; Royal Arch, 67 f; Shrine, and Christian, 83
Oaths, Masonic, 82 ff
Obligation, Odd Fellow, 137 f; Shrine, 112 f
Occultism, in French Masonry, 123
O'Connell, Daniel, and Masonry, 103
Odd Fellows, 4, 9, 11, 133 ff; founding of, 135 f; ladies' auxiliaries, Church ban on, 140; membership of, 135; membership restrictions of, 136; and Negro, 137; pledges of, 137 f
OES, see Eastern Star, Order of,
Oliver, on Masonic history, 13
Opposition to Masonry, Orthodox, 3; Protestant, 3; see also under various church bodies
Organizations, allied Masonic, 110 ff
Orthodox Presbyterian Church, and Masonry, 154

Papal condemnations of Masonry, 100 ff
Patriarchs Militant (IOOF), 137